Jon Sobrino

Archbishop Romero

Memories and Reflections

Translated from the Spanish by
Robert R. Barr

D1508874

ORBIS BOOKS

Maryknoll, New York 10545

Second Printing, May 1990

The Catholic Foreign Mission Society of America (Maryknoll) recruits and trains people for overseas missionary service. Through Orbis Books, Maryknoll aims to foster the international dialogue that is essential to mission. The books published, however, reflect the opinions of their authors and are not meant to represent the official position of the society.

English translation copyright © 1990 by Orbis Books,
Maryknoll, N.Y. 10545
Published in the United States of America by Orbis Books
Manufactured in the United States of America

Library of Congress Cataloguing-in-Publication Data

Sobrino, Jon.
    [Essays. English. Selections]
    Archbishop Romero : memories and reflections / Jon Sobrino ;
translated from the Spanish by Robert R. Barr.
      p. cm.
    Essays originally written in Spanish, 1980-1989.
    ISBN 0-88344-667-7
    1. Romero, Oscar A. (Oscar Arnulfo), 1917-1980. 2. Catholic
Church—El Salvador—History—20th century. 3. El Salvador—Church
history—20th century. 4. Sociology, Christian (Catholic)
5. Liberation theology. 6. Catholic Church—Doctrines—
History—20th century. I. Title.
BX4705.R669S636 1990
282'.092—dc20   89-48221
                                        CIP

To the memory of
Ignacio Ellacuría, S.J.
Ignacio Martín-Baró, S.J.
Amando López, S.J.
Joaquín López y López, S.J.
Segundo Montes, S.J.
Juan Ramón Moreno, S.J.
Julia Elba Ramos
Celina Ramos
murdered in San Salvador on November 16, 1989,
and to all the others who have died in hope of the Kingdom

Gloria Dei, vivens pauper

Contents

PART 2
Archbishop Romero: Witness of God

Preface

Saturday, March 24, 1990, marked the tenth anniversary of the martyrdom of Oscar Arnulfo Romero. The archbishop of San Salvador was shot to death as he was celebrating the eucharist in the chapel of Divine Providence Hospital, where he also maintained his residence.

Everyone must die. But Archbishop Romero's death was not like other deaths. Like the death of Jesus, it was a murder and a martyrdom.

The tenth anniversary of that murder and martyrdom gives us occasion to reflect on the fact that we are under an obligation to Archbishop Romero's memory. To forget him would be ungrateful. "Woe to peoples who forget their martyrs!" Brazilian bishop Pedro Casaldáliga has said. We shall also surely do very well to remember that martyrs give us the light we need to live as Christians and as human beings. The blood of the martyrs — their unconditional love — gives us the courage and strength we shall need if we are to keep up our courage along the hard pathway of life and faith.

I should like to offer this book, then, as a contribution to the commemoration of the tenth anniversary of Archbishop Romero's martyrdom. The book consists of six chapters. Five of the six chapters were written at various times over the past ten years and have appeared in other publications; a few of those pieces have been slightly revised for the present volume. One article (chapter 1) is a new essay, written expressly for presentation here.

I have arranged all of these articles in a particular order, and divided the book into two parts. In Part 1, which will be lengthier and more analytical, I propose to reflect on the figure of Archbishop Romero as a believer, as an archbishop, as a Salvadoran, as a prophet, and as an inspiration for theology. Part 2 will be much shorter, as it will consist simply of two homilies I have preached on the subject of Archbishop Romero, my intent being to synthesize the totality of his person and work — to say, in a few words, what and who Archbishop Oscar Arnulfo Romero actually was and is.

Chapter 1, the essay written expressly for inclusion in this volume, is based on my personal experience and recounts some of my own recollections of Archbishop Romero. A number of considerations have prompted me to open the collection on a personal note. First is my personal gratitude. There is no such thing as gratitude that will not sooner or later come to expression. I feel a need to evince the human warmth of a subject that will be analyzed with more scientific objectivity in subsequent chapters. But I have a second reason, as well, for having written this opening essay. I believe it very important to restate the fact that Archbishop Romero is more than an analyzable concept or a venerable myth. He was someone very real, someone whom "we have seen, heard, and touched," as the first Christians said of Jesus. Recalling him is an important, useful way of reactualizing him — a way of making him real once more. And finally, I have a third reason: with the passing of time, memories become more important for an adequate appreciation of the present. Only half of the population of El Salvador still remember Archbishop Romero in the flesh.

The present volume, then, is a collection of analyses, homilies, and memories. The structural limitation of this arrangement is that each of the chapters will be topical, and hence offers only a partial view of its subject. Thus there is no way to avoid a certain amount of repetition throughout the various chapters. Still I hope and believe that this collection will offer a vision of the essence of Archbishop Oscar Arnulfo Romero, who, in the ten years since his death, has never ceased to inspire and enlighten so many Christians and so many human beings.

In conclusion, I should like to point out that this book is only one of very many testimonials to Archbishop Romero's memory that have appeared in order to commemorate this anniversary. Other contributions will be made in other ways. The poor contribute the most, with their songs and poetry composed in Archbishop Romero's honor, and with all their sufferings and their hopes. After all, it is they who remember him best, and so it is they who can do the most to render him present for us. But I hope that my own recollections and theological reflection will also help keep Oscar Arnulfo Romero alive in our midst.

CHAPTER 1

Some Personal Recollections

I

My first personal encounter with Archbishop Oscar Romero took place on March 12, 1977. In the afternoon of that day, Father Rutilio Grande, S.J., and two *campesinos*, a boy and an old man, had been murdered near El Paisnal. A few hours later, in the Jesuit house at Aguilares, a large number of persons had gathered—we Jesuits, other priests, sisters, and hundreds of *campesinos*, all come to weep for the two murdered *campesinos* and for Rutilio, the priest who had proclaimed to us the good news of the gospel.

We had been awaiting the arrival of Archbishop Romero, installed as head of the Archdiocese of San Salvador less than three weeks before, on February 22, and of his auxiliary, Bishop Rivera. The bishops would lead our concelebration of the first eucharist in the presence of the remains of the three murder victims. But it was growing late, and the prelates had not yet arrived. The people were beginning to show a certain impatience and uneasiness, especially now that night was falling. So Father Jerez, Provincial of the Jesuits of Central America, decided to begin the celebration of the eucharist without them; and all except myself—I no longer remember why—began to move toward the church, which was attached to the house. Suddenly there was a knock at the door. I went to the door, opened it, and there stood Archbishop Romero and Bishop Rivera. The archbishop looked very serious and concerned. I greeted our visitors, and without another word led them to the church.

This was my very first personal contact with Archbishop Romero. It was of course a very brief, purely symbolic encounter. But the occasion rendered it one of immense personal significance for me. At the moment, obviously, all our thoughts were on Rutilio and the two *campesinos*, the murder victims. It had occurred to all of us what might be in store. True, the repression of the *campesinos* had been mounted long since. And a number of priests had been arrested and expelled from the country. But for a priest to be murdered in El Salvador was unheard-of. Now it was no longer merely the rules of fair play that were being broken; treachery itself had taken hold. Anything could happen in the country if the powerful had dared to murder a priest. And 1977 would indeed prove a difficult year for *campesinos*, priests, and us Jesuits. Two months after Rutilio's murder, the three remaining Jesuits in Aguilares were expelled from the country. On June 20, all of us Jesuits received death threats.

Uppermost on our minds that night, then, was the dead body of Rutilio. But I was also mightily struck by the serious, preoccupied face of Archbishop Romero. Here was an ecclesiastic of whom I had heard only that he was very conservative, and not really very courageous. And here he was, beginning his archiepiscopal ministry not amidst a series of solemn celebrations, but awash in arrests, torture, the expulsion of priests, and now, suddenly, the blood of Rutilio Grande, one of the priests with whom he had been on the most familiar terms. Who could have foretold that the growing repression of *campesinos* and laborers, which the Salvadoran bishops, at the insistence of Bishop Rivera in particular, had so courageously denounced in their message of March 5, would so quickly come to this?

From that night on, my mental image of Archbishop Romero's serious, concerned face when I opened the door was like a magnet to me, attracting me to him and overwhelming me with the idea that I must somehow help him. Actually, the preconception we had had of him had already been somewhat modified, as in the course of the clergy meetings of the closing days of February, where he was introduced as our new archbishop; at that time he had asked our help in the serious difficulties he was sure to encounter. My decision to try to help him was an enthusiastic one, then, and it was shared by many. It was also something we all perceived as a matter of urgency, since we all expected things to get very difficult in the immediate future, and we knew that we would do much better if we faced them united as a church rather than in a state of separation and division. And so there had already been a noticeable change in the relationship between Archbishop Romero and ourselves. But that night of March 12 sealed that relationship.

To tell the truth, the change was a surprising one. For one thing, my little contact with him had been rather tense since I had returned to El Salvador in 1974. And the one thing I knew for certain about Archbishop Romero was that he had been a very conservative auxiliary, much under the influence of Opus Dei, and an adversary of priests and bishops who had accepted the Medellín line; sometimes he had gone to the point of accusing these bishops and priests of "false ideology." He also regarded several Salvadoran Jesuits as "Marxist" and "politicized," and these were precisely the persons under whose guidance I was taking my first steps as a Jesuit and theologian after a seven years' absence from the country.

The first time I ever laid eyes on Archbishop Romero, if my memory serves me correctly, was in 1974, at the seminary of San José de la Montaña, where I was giving a talk to priests and seminarians on the historical Jesus and the Reign of God. In the front row, to my right, sat Archbishop Luis Chávez, along with Bishop Rivera, his auxiliary, and Bishop Romero, then likewise his auxiliary. What impressed me that evening about Bishop Romero was that, apparently, at least, he was there only out of a sense of duty to his archbishop. He never raised his head to look at me all during the time I spoke. It was as if he wished to show that he did not endorse what I was saying, but, precisely, was taking his distance from it. In a word, I must have been another of those "Marxist priests." And I, for my part, was convinced that Bishop Romero was exactly as he had been portrayed.

My worst suspicions were confirmed on August 6, 1976, when our country celebrated its patronal Feast of Our Lord Jesus Christ the Divine Savior, and the customary Solemn High Mass was celebrated in the Metropolitan Cathedral of San Salvador. In those years a well-known priest or ecclesiastic would be invited to pronounce a solemn homily on that day, in the presence of all of the bishops, government officials, the diplomatic corps, and so on. It was an important address, then. It certainly had been in 1970 (if I may be permitted a little digression), when the homilist had been Father Grande, so respected and loved in the archdiocese, and a candidate for appointment as rector of the seminary. Rutilio had divided his homily according to the three words on the Salvadoran flag: *Dios, Unión, Libertad* — "God, Unity, Freedom." His homily consisted of a resounding denunciation of the condition of the country. With the latter two elements in the Salvadoran motto missing, said Rutilio, so was the first! As there was no unity or freedom among us, we were without God. This had caused a great deal of surprise, and a great stir. And Rutilio had not been appointed rector of the seminary.

In 1976, then, the homilist chosen for the occasion had been Bishop Romero, then bishop of Santiago de María. I did not attend the Mass that August 6, but a few hours after its conclusion a fellow priest brought me a tape of the homily. I turned on the recorder, and chills went up my spine. Bishop Romero's first point was a criticism of the christologies being developed in El Salvador — "rationalistic, revolutionary, hate-filled christologies." Bishop Romero had begun his homily with a virulent criticism of my own christology!

Understandably, then, many of us priests and others were anything but enthusiastic over the prospect of Bishop Romero's succeeding Archbishop Luis Chávez. Chávez had been a pastoral bishop, very close to the people, and we had been on very good terms with him. To my mind the ideal candidate would have been Bishop Rivera. But it was not to be. Returning to El Salvador on a flight from Mexico City on February 8, I saw a large photograph of Bishop Romero on the cover of a Salvadoran magazine. The new archbishop of San Salvador was Bishop Romero. Bad times in store, I thought. I wondered if Archbishop Romero would have the courage to denounce repression, or if on the contrary he would abet it — if he would defend the threatened *campesinos* and priests, or leave them in the lurch. A few days later I received a post card from a Mexican Jesuit that might as well have been a letter of condolence. As a matter of fact, we all thought we faced a very bleak future. Fortunately, we were all mistaken.

The things I am recounting now, of course, seemed of scant importance that night of March 12. The homily of August 6 was the furthest thing from either of our minds, Archbishop Romero's or my own. But in thinking it over afterwards, it seemed to me that that first, silent greeting had been a kind of reconciliation with Archbishop Romero—the beginning of a new ecclesial relationship and a new friendship. I know that many of my colleagues thought the same, and we were all glad. Some people think that the only thing forward-looking priests, liberation theologians, and base communities are after is tactical relations with the hierarchy. But this is not true. For all of us it is a joy to live in the church as brothers and sisters, including, and especially—when it is possible—with those brothers of ours who are also our bishops.

But about that same time, another thought began to haunt me. I knew that Archbishop Romero generally had the humility and delicacy to apologize for behavior he regretted. He had come to a base community to ask forgiveness, years after the fact, for what he had said to them in 1972, when he practically justified the militarization of the national university and the ensuing repression. He had also asked forgiveness of a fellow Jesuit of mine who had been rector of the seminary when the bishops— among them, most definitely, Archbishop Romero—decided to take the seminary away from the Jesuits. This was typical of his humility and delicacy. I do not know why, but for some reason I was obsessed by the notion that one day Archbishop Romero would feel badly for his attacks on me, and apologize. Happily, I never spoke of this. If I had, I think I should have been even more haunted by the idea. At all events, one day—I think it was toward the end of April 1977—Archbishop Romero saw me in a corner of the cathedral and came to speak to me. "Thank you," he told me, "for your reflections on the church. I think it helped a great deal." He was referring to the dossier he had taken to Rome to explain the situation in our country and the changed behavior of the church after Rutilio's death. I had done some of the work on the theological part of the report. Actually there was no need for Archbishop Romero to thank me or any of the many others who had placed ourselves at his service. But I certainly appreciated the gesture. It meant a kind of ecclesial acceptance of what we were doing. Especially, it was a demonstration of confidence. Archbishop Romero always had this delicacy. Whenever I had helped him in some way, in publishing the documents of Medellín and Puebla, for example, or with any theological reflections I might write for his use, Archbishop Romero would send me a letter or little note of thanks.

II

But to go back to that night of March 12: after Mass, Archbishop Romero asked us priests and sisters to remain in the church. Some of the *campesinos* stayed too, and naturally we made no discrimination. And we held a planning session right then and there, in the late hours of the night, without waiting for the next day or a night's rest. Archbishop Romero was visibly agitated. He seemed to be laboring under the responsibility of having to do something and not knowing exactly what to do. After all, the problem facing him was unheard-of. And the question he asked us was elementary. What should we and could we do, as church, about Rutilio's murder?

Agitated, perturbed, still he was ready to do whatever would be necessary, and I could see this. He must have been afraid, however. The hour had come in which he would have to face up to the powerful—the oligarchy and the government. I shall never forget how totally sincere he was in asking for our help— how his words came from the heart. An archbishop was actually asking us to help him—persons whom a few weeks before he had regarded as suspect, as Marxist! This gesture of dialogue and humility made me very happy. And I reflected that, while the tragedy of that day seemed such an inauspicious beginning for Archbishop Romero in his new, archiepiscopal responsibility, actually it could be a most auspicious one. The seed of a united, determined, and clear-sighted church, a church which would one day grow to be so great, had been sown. I felt great tenderness for that humble bishop, who was asking us, practically begging us, to help him bear the burden that heaven had imposed on him, a far heavier burden than his shoulders, or anyone else's, could ever have borne alone.

I also felt, or seemed to surmise, that something very profound was transpiring deep within Archbishop Romero. Surely he was uneasy. But in the midst of his uneasiness in those first moments, with all of his hesitancy about what to do, I think he was forming the high resolve to react in whatever way God might ask: he was making an authentic option for the poor, who had been represented, a scant hour before, by hundreds of *campesinos* gathered about three corpses, helpless in the face of the repression they had already suffered and knowing full well that there was more to come. I do not know whether I am correctly interpreting what was actually transpiring in Archbishop Romero's heart at these moments, but I believe he must have felt that those *campesinos* had made an option for him—that they were asking him to defend them. And his response was to make an option for the *campesinos*—to be converted and transformed into their defender, to become the voice of the voiceless. I believe that Archbishop Romero's definitive conversion began that night.

Actually Archbishop Romero did not particularly like to hear his change referred to as a conversion. And he had a point. He used to recall his humble origins. He had never known anything like wealth or abundance. His family had led a life of poverty and austerity. And of course it was universally acknowledged that his life as a priest and bishop had been one of outstanding virtue. In his own way, he had been open to the poor. He had defended them in Santiago de María at a moment when they were suffering cruel repression. No one, then, regarded Archbishop Romero as an evil, irresponsible, or deceitful person. Even in his most conservative period, his ethical stature encouraged his subordinates to feel free to speak with him of the most delicate matters. I believe, then, that Archbishop Romero had always had a heart that was pure, and an ethical reserve that not even his conservative ideology, or the backward, reactionary behavior of a goodly part of the national hierarchy to which he belonged, could succeed in stifling. What had happened is that his inner personhood had been divided in two. In his heart he maintained authentic religious ideals, and accepted the directives of Vatican II and Medellín in principle. But he interpreted the novelty of the council and Medellín from a very conservative posture, with fear of anything that might possibly immerse the church in the conflictive, ambiguous flesh of history. It was this interior division, I believe, that dissolved that night, and I believe that this phenomenon can be called a conversion — not so much in the sense of ceasing to do evil and beginning to do good, but in the sense of grasping the will of God and being determined to implement it, and this in the spirit of deep, radical change. The will of God must have looked very different to Archbishop Romero that night in the presence of those three dead bodies and with hundreds of *campesinos* staring at him wondering what he was going to do about what had happened.

Whether one actually calls it a conversion or not, the radical change that took place in Archbishop Romero on the occasion of Rutilio's murder was one of the most impressive things anyone around him, including myself, had ever seen. He was fifty-nine years old at the time, an age at which people's psychological and mental structure, their understanding of the faith, their spirituality, and their Christian commitment have typically hardened. Furthermore, he had just been named an archbishop — the highest level of responsibility in the institutional church, which, like any other institution, necessarily has a strong instinct for continuity and prudence, not to say out-and-out retrenchment. Finally, historical circumstances were scarcely favorable. Archbishop Romero was altogether aware, from the outset, that he had been the candidate of the right. He had known the cajolery of the powerful from the start. They would build him a magnificent bishop's palace, they told him, and they hoped he would reverse the line taken by his predecessor, Luis Chávez y González. But Archbishop Romero changed, and changed radically. He refused the beautiful palace and went to live in Divine Providence Hospital, in a little room next to the sacristy. Thus not only were the powers cheated of their hopes for a nice, pliable ecclesiastical puppet, but the new archbishop was actually going to oppose them somehow. In store for him, of course, if he did so, was the wrath of the mighty — the oligarchy, the government, the political parties, the army, the security forces, and later, the majority of his brother bishops, various Vatican offices, and even the U.S. government. In the balance of forces operating in the background of his conversion, Archbishop Romero had in his favor a group of priests and nuns, and, especially, the suffering and hope of a whole people. Against him was everyone with any power. Evangelically, then, the balance of forces was in his favor; but naturally speaking, it was against him. If Archbishop Romero set out on new paths, at his age, in his place at the pinnacle of the institution, and against such odds, then his conversion must have been very real. It must have reached the deepest corners of his being, shaping him for good and all, and leading him to the sacrifice of his life. His external change in behavior—an undeniable change, acknowledged by all—must have been the result of a very deep, very real interior change.

What was the cause of Archbishop Romero's conversion? I have been asked this question countless times. I have no "objective," psychological answer, nor did I ever speak of this with him personally. It is not easy to plumb the depths of another, and of course it would be presumptuous to claim to be able to. Still I should like to set forth my own view of Archbishop Romero's conversion, be it only to show that the interior change of which I speak actually did take place, and that his external behavior is not to be ascribed to any sort of "manipulation."

I believe that the murder of Rutilio Grande was the occasion of the conversion of Archbishop Romero—as well as being a source of light and courage to follow his new paths. Archbishop Romero had known Rutilio, and held him in such high regard that he invited him to serve as master of ceremonies at his episcopal consecration. He did not, however, approve of Rutilio's pastoral ministry at Aguilares. It seemed too political to him, too "horizontal," foreign to the church's basic mission, and dangerously close to revolutionary ideas. Rutilio had been a problem for Archbishop Romero, then. In fact he was an enigma. Here was a virtuous, zealous, deeply believing priest. Yet this admirable priest's approach to the pastoral ministry was one which, at least in Archbishop Romero's eyes, was simply incorrect and mistaken. It was this enigma, I think, that was solved the day Rutilio died. I think that, as Archbishop Romero stood

gazing at the mortal remains of Rutilio Grande, the scales fell
from his eyes. Rutilio had been right! The kind of pastoral activity, the kind of church, the kind of faith he had advocated
had been the right kind after all. And then, on an even deeper
level: if Rutilio had died as Jesus died, if he had shown that
greatest of all love, the love required to lay down one's very life
for others—was this not because his life and mission had been
like the life and mission of Jesus? Far from being a deluded,
misled follower of Jesus, Rutilio must have been an exemplary
one! Ah, then it had not been Rutilio, but Oscar who had been
mistaken! It had not been Rutilio who ought to have changed,
but himself, Oscar Romero. And Archbishop Romero translated
these reflections, which theoretically could have remained in the
state of pure ratiocination, into a decision to change—a determination to live and act as Rutilio had, and above all, as Jesus
had. In the presence of Rutilio's dead body, Archbishop Romero
had felt what St. Ignatius Loyola felt in his contemplation on
sin, when in the eyes of his imagination he stood before Christ
crucified. There the question comes thundering in, down to the
deepest recesses of one's being: "What will I do for Christ?" I
believe that it was Rutilio's death that gave Archbishop Romero
the strength for new activity. It "shook him up," as we say. Now
Rutilio's life gave Archbishop Romero the fundamental direction for his own life. Of course, Rutilio had been a simple missionary priest, and not archbishop of San Salvador, and could
not have given examples of the concrete expressions of this new
fundamental direction that would be appropriate for the archbishop of San Salvador. It was up to Oscar Romero to find these
concrete expressions himself, in function of his particular, critical historical circumstances. Archbishop Romero's conversion
used to be referred to in those days as "Rutilio's miracle."

A second thing that must have had a prompt impact on Archbishop Romero in those first days was the different reactions of
various elements in the church. He was well aware that his appointment had not been well received by priests who practiced
a more forward-moving pastoral ministry, by the base communities, or by anyone whose work was one of consciousness-raising
and liberation in the spirit of Medellín. He knew it had filled
these persons with fear. He also knew of the jubilation that his

appointment had inspired among comfortable Catholics—those who had been known to connive with the power groups that had attacked and calumniated his predecessor, Archbishop Chávez—and even among a little group of priests who had cozied up to those power groups. And so Archbishop Romero must have been very surprised when, in those first, so difficult days, when he saw that he was going to have to take real risks, the first group rallied to him and the second abandoned him. In the hour of truth, those whom he had regarded with suspicion, had attacked, and even out and out condemned, were with him. The others, whom he had regarded as devout and orthodox, so prudent and "nonpolitical," apparently so faithful to whatever the church had to say, left him in the lurch, as Jesus' disciples had their master, and promptly began to criticize, attack, and disobey him, thereby showing their true colors: their apparent loyalty to the hierarchy did not go so far as to agree with their archbishop when he said things no longer to their liking, or when their particular interests were somehow threatened.

I believe that all of this gave Archbishop Romero a great deal of food for thought. Not that everything the forward-looking priests did was perfect. But at least they were persons of far more truth and Christian love than were others. Whatever might be the theological and political ideas of the former—Archbishop Romero clearly saw—at least they were determined to stand up for him in his denunciation of the barbarity of his country, which showed that they were honest about the tragedy of Salvadoran reality, unlike the others, who ignored it and attempted to make excuses for it. And they were willing to run personal risks, speak out, make public denunciations, although now this would mean that they would be branded as unpatriotic and un-Christian, arrested, and even murdered. Archbishop Romero found this minimal truth and commitment in a good-sized group of priests and nuns, and did not find it in the other little group. The latter fell silent, and attempted to justify its silence, as Archbishop Romero himself had done some months earlier, with an appeal to the "good of the church." By way of one tragic example, we might recall the circular letter of Cardinal Mario Casariego of Guatemala to his priests, in which he said that it was Rutilio Grande's own fault that he had been murdered, that he had been meddling in matters that were of no concern to him, and that the priests of Guatemala would do well not to follow his example.

This kind of reaction had a great impact on Archbishop Romero. I recall how, one evening a few days after Rutilio's murder, at YSAX—the archdiocesan radio station, which was to become so well-known for its rebroadcasts of Archbishop Romero's homilies, as well as for having been repeatedly dynamited—he showed me a letter he had received. Written on elaborate stationery, with a floral motif if I remember correctly, it had been sent by someone who had been close to Archbishop Romero, but who now expressed surprise at the change that had come over him, and disapproval of his new behavior. Archbishop Romero showed not the slightest perturbation, I recall, but simply murmured to me: "Opus Dei." What I think he was saying is that here was someone who had no more understanding than he himself had once had.

Thus what the two sides did or did not do in those days helped Archbishop Romero acquire a clearer view of things, and this in turn helped him change. In sum, we might say: in times of national crisis, you cannot simply keep repeating that you are a Christian, and forget about history. You cannot hide in a "Christianity" that will exempt you from the obligation of being a citizen of your country. Those who had simply abandoned El Salvador to its fate under the pretext of being Christians no longer shed any light as far as Archbishop Romero was concerned. Those who had made an option for their country, by telling the truth, by denouncing atrocities, by making a commitment to justice—albeit with limitations and exaggerations—now became Archbishop Romero's guiding light.

A third factor in Archbishop Romero's conversion—the definitive factor, the one that kept him faithful to God's will to the end—was his people, a people of the poor. The poor very promptly showed him their acceptance, support, affection, and love. Surely he did not expect this when he was appointed archbishop. But the poor certainly hoped for an archbishop such as he proved to be. And the fact is, as I have already remarked, that in El Salvador, as in so many other places in Latin America, before the church made an option for the poor, the poor had made an option for the church. They had found no one else to defend them, not in the government, not in the armed forces, not in the political parties, and not in private enterprise.

While Archbishop Romero was taking his first steps, making his first denunciations, making his first visits to the base communities, the poor fairly swarmed around him. He took them to his heart, and they were there to stay. And they took him to their own hearts, where he has remained to this day.

I do not propose to belabor this abundantly acknowledged, public, point. I only wish to add that Archbishop Romero must have found in the poor what the prophet Isaiah contemplated in the Suffering Servant of Yahweh, and St. Paul saw in the crucified Christ: light and salvation. The suffering of the poor must have shaken Archbishop Romero to his depths as he watched their oppression swell to such intolerable proportions. The poor were effectively calling for his conversion. But in offering him light and salvation, they also facilitated that conversion. And Archbishop Romero recognized this. For me there is no doubt that this is Archbishop Romero's last secret, and I shall reveal that secret. In one of his most felicitous expressions, in words of the kind that cannot be invented, but can only come from the heart, he said: "With this people, it is not difficult to be a good shepherd."

III

In the immediate aftermath of Rutilio's murder, the archdiocesan chancery, indeed, the whole archdiocese, saw moments of great perturbation and turmoil—moments that marked out for Archbishop Romero a path he would walk to the end without ever looking back. He understood very soon that, as archbishop, he must clarify for the people the nature of the church—explain its prophetic denunciation and its defense of the poor. And in his very first year among us he wrote two pastoral letters on the church.

Archbishop Romero put these great convictions, that had begun to come together in his mind, to work. During those same first days he published a series of communiqués denouncing the repression of the people and the persecution of the church, demanding the government investigate the murders, and promising the people that the church would be on their side. He defended the people, denouncing injustices, cost what it might, be it the blood of its priests. Most dramatically—and in contravention of long years of tradition—Archbishop Romero publicly promised that he would participate in no official government function until these crimes had been solved and the repression had been stopped. And he kept his promise. For three years he never participated in governmental functions. He was unwilling to bestow on a government like ours the blessing of his presence.

Thus Archbishop Romero's very first acts provided a preview of what the *modus procedendi* of his pastoral mission among us would be. He engaged the clergy, the sisters, and the laity in dialogue, and then decided what to do. I remember a meeting during those first days that lasted from eight in the morning until eight at night. Archbishop Romero was a prophet from the beginning, as he forthrightly denounced the abuses perpetrated by the oppressor. He was evangelical, and in all simplicity: he refused to be frightened by the political consequences of his actions. And he was all of this publicly, speaking to the country, and making specific promises—promises that he could be held to, promises he could be called on to keep if he were not keeping them already.

Among the promises he made, and then kept, two stand out especially in those days: the suspension of classes for three days in all Catholic schools; and the single Mass of March 20. The suspension of classes was not a vacation, as his detractors protested, but three days of study, reflection, and prayer—three days spent with the Bible, Vatican II, and Medellín. I remember how rapidly we worked to select passages from all three sources to be used in this reflection.

The single Mass caused an even greater flurry of excitement and comment, and I think that this decision had important consequences for Archbishop Romero's own interior life. It forced him to come to grips with his own faith, and with the church institution as well. The government was opposed to the single Mass, to be held in the Metropolitan Cathedral, fearing a massive concentration of people, as indeed was to be the case. And it was the Catholics of the wealthy plantations who hypocritically complained that they would be deprived of the opportunity to hear Mass and fulfill their Sunday obligation! It seems not to have occurred to them that they could attend Mass more easily than anyone else — simply by driving to the cathedral — although, admittedly, they would have had to stand among the poor in the sun for three hours. But even Archbishop Romero had had his doubts at first about the single Mass. He was convinced that something dramatic had to be done to stun the country and shake it from its apathy. But he had a theological scruple, which he formulated at our meeting with characteristic sincerity. "If the eucharist gives glory to God," he asked, "will not God have more glory in the usual number of Sunday Masses than in just one?"

I must confess that my heart sank to hear him. Here was a theology straight out of the dark ages. But in thinking it over afterwards, and on the basis of all his actions, I finally came to interpret Archbishop Romero's words correctly. He was only showing his deep, genuine interest in the things of God. His theology was questionable. Beyond question, however, was his profound faith in God, and his surpassing concern for the glory of God in this world.

With the same frank attitude with which Archbishop Romero had propounded his own difficulty, others of us explained our theological reasoning to the contrary. A lengthy discussion ensued. Finally Father Jerez spoke up: "I think Monseñor is absolutely right to be concerned for the glory of God. But unless I am mistaken, the Fathers of the Church said, '*Gloria Dei, vivens homo*' — the glory of God is the living person." Father Jerez's intervention decided the issue for all practical purposes. Archbishop Romero seemed convinced, and relieved of his scruple. And he decided on the single Mass for that particular Sunday.

At the moment, I thought only that Archbishop Romero had made a lucid, courageous pastoral decision. But afterwards I thought what it must have meant for him to accept such a novel formulation of what the actual "glory of God" is. At stake had been nothing less than his personal understanding of God — his faith in God. It was not a mere matter of a new theological formulation. It was a matter of a new understanding of God.

And Archbishop Romero had accepted that new understanding. Tirelessly he would repeat that nothing was more important to God than the life of the poor. When he went to Puebla, he met Leonardo Boff there, and told him: "In my country, people are being horribly murdered. We must defend the minimum gift of God, which is also the maximum: life." He himself reformulated Saint Irenaeus's aphorism, the one Father Jerez had cited, as, " *'Gloria Dei, vivens pauper'* — the glory of God is the living poor person." Conversely, he railed against the idols — those false, but real, divinities that deal in death, the deities that call for victims because they live on their blood as the only means to their own survival.

I believe that Archbishop Romero, at the age of fifty-nine, not only underwent a conversion, but had a new experience of God. Never again would he be capable of separating God from the poor, or his faith in God from his defense of the poor. I believe he saw in God the prototype of his own option for the poor, and that that prototype demanded he put his option into practice. But I think his experience also enlightened him as to who God is. Why was he never shocked by new formulations of God's identity? He assimilated concepts like "God of life, God of the Reign, God of the poor," and so on, altogether naturally. He was particularly fond of the Gloria of the *Misa Salvadoreña,* which sings the praise of the God of life and condemns the gods of power and money.

However, this costly, gladsome discovery of the God of the poor never induced Archbishop Romero to disparage in the least something I think must have been a constant in every aspect of his life: the mystery of God. From his new starting point in the poor, Archbishop Romero discovered that God is theirs — their defender, their liberator. Among the poor he discovered that God is God become small — a suffering God, a crucified God. But this also led him to sound the depths of the mystery of an ever greater, transcendent God, the last reserve of truth, goodness, and humanity, on whom we human beings can rely. I do not know whether Archbishop Romero knew the words from Irenaeus that immediately follow those cited by Father Jerez. *"Vita autem hominis, visio Dei,"* Irenaeus continues: "And the life of the human being is the vision of God." But whether he knew the words or not, he communicated their content. Personally, I was profoundly struck—and I have tried to convey it in my writings—by his faith in God, his absolute conviction of God's reality, his utter conviction that the mystery of God is salvific for human beings, that it is good that there is a God, that we should be glad there is a God. On February 10, 1980, in a situation that had become chaotic, in out-and-out confrontation with the government, the army, the oligarchy, and the United States, Archbishop Romero was once more the courageous, implacable prophet, speaking of the things of this world and coming out in defense of an oppressed people. But in the same homily, and just as naturally as he had pronounced his historic denunciations, he spoke the following words: "Tell me, beloved brothers and sisters, that the fruit of today's sermon will be that each of us will encounter God, and that we shall live in the glory of his majesty and our littleness! . . . No human being has self-knowledge without having encountered God."

To be able to utter these words is to have had a profound experience of God. In God's name Archbishop Romero defended the life of the poor. And when he sought to give all of us the best he had to give, he gave us simply God.

The God of the poor and the mystery of God are what Archbishop Romero made present to all who were willing to listen. In El Salvador he restored respect for God. The poor listened to him, of course—what else is left to them, frequently, but their faith in God? But nonbelievers listened to him, as well—those who at least respect God's name. And doubters listened to him, with gratitude that he was shedding light on something that had become darkness for them.

Thanks to Archbishop Romero, our country never hears the fateful reproach so frequently addressed to God's people in Holy Scripture: "On your account the name of God is blasphemed among the nations." But there is more. Italo López Vallecillos, the celebrated Salvadoran author, now deceased, once told me: "I have always pondered the mystery of God. When I was small, it was my grandmother who got me to think about it. Now this mystery has become present to me in Archbishop Romero."

IV

It was this immense faith of Archbishop Romero's, ever ancient and ever new, that was in gestation during those days. No one ever dared ask him, "In what God do you believe?" But the question arose spontaneously when Archbishop Romero conceived the notion of having just one Mass in the archdiocese, in the Metropolitan Cathedral, on the Sunday following Rutilio's death. His decision to schedule the single Mass was the expression of a new faith. No matter that, on the surface, it might have seemed only a courageous pastoral decision to some, a political provocation to others.

But that decision also meant a first serious confrontation between Archbishop Romero and certain echelons of the church institution. And he suffered from this confrontation throughout his three remaining years.

The commotion occasioned by his announcement of the one Mass that Sunday was such that he decided to pay a personal visit to the apostolic nuncio to explain his action. He invited several priests to accompany him, and I was among their number. The nuncio was not in, and we were received by his secretary. It was obvious from the outset that the secretary was annoyed about the single Mass, and he made no effort to conceal his annoyance, although he was a simple monsignor and was addressing the archbishop of San Salvador himself. And so I experienced a little of the authoritarianism so frequently present in "curias" of all kind, civil and ecclesiastical, and their lack of understanding of the suffering of the people — or even that of an archbishop overwhelmed by heavy responsibilities. Rarely, I think, have I felt such indignation as I felt at that moment.

The secretary began by saying that the pastoral and theological argumentation in favor of the single Mass was good. I think he even said that it was very good. This surprised me, since in my naiveté I did not see how such laudatory words could be reconciled with his visible annoyance. "But," he added, "you have forgotten the most important thing."

I could not think what "the most important thing" might be apart from, precisely, pastoral or theological considerations. But the monsignor went on, solemnly: "You have overlooked the canonical aspect." I could scarcely believe my ears. Nor could anyone else. I remarked that nothing was more important than the body of Christ, and that this body was being bled dry in our country; that nothing was more important for the church at this moment than to denounce repression and give the people some hope; and that canonical considerations are secondary in a spiritual emergency. And I reminded him of what Jesus had said about the "sabbath being for man." All was in vain, however, and we had to abandon all levels of the discussion except the canonical. Fortunately, some of the priests with us were able to show the nuncio's secretary that Archbishop Romero had acted correctly even from the standpoint of canon law. I do not think the monsignor was actually convinced, but at least it ended the discussion.

It was a long, unpleasant hour. What impressed me most, however, was that Archbishop Romero was perfectly silent all through the meeting. It was as if he were absent from all of this nit-picking, thinking more of Rutilio's corpse, murdered *campesinos*, and the people's fear and sorrow. At the end of the meeting, however—without raising his voice, and without entering into any discussion of the arguments—he said something like: "Our country is in a very dangerous, extraordinary state. The church must make some equally extraordinary response in terms of denunciation and evangelization. I am responsible for the archdiocese. We shall have the one Mass." That was all that he said. And we left the nunciature. I was still very perturbed. Archbishop Romero radiated serenity and peace. "They do not understand," he told me laconically.

On Sunday, March 20, we concelebrated the only Mass in the archdiocese that day, and it was an unprecedented pastoral success. Cathedral Square was packed. Tens of thousands prayed, sang, received communion, and took courage, the courage of Christian faith and hope. Before Mass several of us heard confessions. A number of penitents told me that this was the first time in a number of years that they had come to confession, and that they had felt the need to come back to God after what had happened to Rutilio. Even in terms of the traditional criterion of number of confessions, the single Mass was a magnificent pastoral achievement. But the nunciature never understood.

This Mass was the beginning of Archbishop Romero's long Calvary of hierarchical misunderstanding and rejection. True, in May 1977 the Salvadoran bishops published a message that could still be interpreted as an expression of support for him. But from that moment on, at any rate, he had nothing but difficulties with the Salvadoran bishops and some of the Vatican offices. Of the former, only Bishop Rivera remained loyal to him.

It is difficult to see how anyone of good will and sound judgment could question Archbishop Romero's loyalty to the church, Vatican II, Medellín and Puebla, the teachings of the popes, and the social teaching of the church. His homilies and pastoral letters draw so abundantly on all of these fonts. One of his greatest joys was to be able to go to Rome to see the Holy Father, tell him about the situation in the country and the Salvadoran church, and receive from him direction and encouragement, or admonitions if need be. He prized his communion with Rome very highly. I recall his jubilation on his return from his first visit to Paul VI, who had squeezed his hands and said, "*Coraggio!*" (Courage!). He also returned satisfied with his second visit to John Paul II, although, as he recounts in his diary, the first one had saddened and disappointed him: apparently misinformed, the Holy Father had failed really to understand him very well. I personally believe that John Paul II evolved in his estimation of Archbishop Romero. At all events, he eventually praised him, publicly, as a pastor and martyr who had given his life for the love of God and the service of his brothers and sisters.

Throughout the course of Archbishop Romero's three years at our head, he likewise had to face the opposition of the Salvadoran bishops themselves, who criticized him both in public and in harsh private reports to the Vatican. At Puebla, Bishop Aparicio publicly accused us Jesuits of being part of the cause of the violence in the country (and this in the presence of Father General Arrupe), and then declared to certain journalists that Archbishop Romero was acting irresponsibly and endangering the entire church, by bringing it into confrontation with the government—adding that he was doing all of this out of vanity, in the hope of becoming "the Latin American Jimmy Carter"! The Vatican sent Archbishop Romero three apostolic visitors in the course of a year and a half—to the astonishment of Salvadorans, who wondered when even one apostolic visitor would be sent to another diocese that had drawn up no pastoral plan, or whose bishop had publicly endorsed the acts of a criminal army.

In Rome, Archbishop Romero's relations with Cardinal Baggio were very tense. The cardinal spoke to him of the possibility that an apostolic administrator, with full powers, might be appointed for our archdiocese. Whereupon Archbishop Romero only asked that this be done in a dignified way, to spare the people any suffering, although he added that he did not think it would be the thing to do. On one occasion Cardinal Baggio received him in his study with: "You are in bad company," and showed him a book he had on his writing stand. The book, published by the University of Central America, contained Archbishop Romero's Third Pastoral Letter and Bishop Rivera's first. On the cover were the names of Ignacio Ellacuría, T. R. Campos, and Jon Sobrino.

And so Archbishop Romero discovered—unfortunately, when he least expected it—the limitations, intrigues, and pettiness of the church institution. It was extremely painful to him that, with his country screaming in agony, and with priests being murdered, the church institution offered him not support but opposition—that with the Reign of God itself at stake, the concern of the Salvadoran bishops was that nothing untoward befall the institution. This caused him a great deal of suffering, and in his last months he felt a real distaste for the meetings of the Salvadoran Bishops Conference, where two completely different languages were spoken.

During the last retreat he was ever to make, a month before his assassination, he wrote out, in his own hand, a list of the things that most concerned him, and that he had spoken to his spiritual director, Father Azcue, S.J., by way of part of his preparation for a spiritual conference. One of the concerns he listed was "my clashes with my brothers in the episcopacy." He must have emerged from his talk with Father Azcue much heartened, since he then wrote:

The following consideration has given me a great deal of confidence. They criticize my pastoral actions. Very well, then what alternative do they propose? And this reflection has confirmed my conviction that the only important thing is the radicality of the gospel — something not everyone can understand. I can give in on incidental points, but I cannot yield when what is at stake is a radical following of the gospel. This radicality has always been met with opposition — and painful division.

In the midst of his suffering, Archbishop Romero found strength and relief in his faith. He was also buoyed up by the people's immense affection for him. Finally, he was consoled — as he recounts in his diary — by his conversations in Rome with Cardinal Pironio and Father Arrupe ("a saint," the diary calls the latter), as well as with Cardinal Aloísio Lorscheider on the occasion of the latter's visit to El Salvador. But the cross weighed very heavy on him. We could see this quite clearly at Puebla.

I went to Puebla, as did other theologians and social scientists, in order to be able to follow this important conference more closely, and to speak with the bishops who had asked our help. (We had not been invited to participate officially.) One evening our group met with a considerable number of bishops, who had come to our quarters to confer on certain theological matters. Together we considered the main themes of Puebla, together we dined, and together we prayed. Archbishop Romero was there. He looked happy, and was obviously enjoying himself. Lecture halls were not the "natural place" for someone like him. He liked being among the *campesinos*, and at Puebla he felt more at ease with journalists, speaking with them about El Salvador, than in the corridors of Palafox Seminary with its atmosphere of church politics and diplomacy. Toward the end of our meeting, someone suggested that the bishops at Puebla — whoever among them might so desire — send joint letters of encouragement and support to the bishops of the most afflicted churches of Central America: those of El Salvador, Guatemala, and Nicaragua. The letters to El Salvador and Nicaragua were written, and several bishops signed them. The Guatemalan bishops present at the meeting judged it more prudent to decline this public demonstration of solidarity. I remember how moved Archbishop Romero was, by everything, by the fellowship and communion of the meeting, by the sincerity of our discussions, by the atmosphere of faith and church, and especially by the affection and solidarity of his fellow bishops. Almost in tears he said, "I felt like a brother among my brother bishops."

V

These are my principal recollections of Archbishop Romero in his first months as our ordinary, together with some observations on the later course of events in his life. In sum, I think Archbishop Romero underwent a process of conversion, and that, relatively quickly, he found the new route that he would travel to the end. I do not actually know how much time it took him to find this new road. I do not know whether his conversion was like St. Paul's, sudden as a fall from a horse, or like the more gradual experience of a discernment of the movement of spirits, of which St. Ignatius Loyola tells. But a very few months after his appointment, Archbishop Romero had become a very special bishop, Christian, and Salvadoran.

In a brief time, Archbishop Romero had to learn to make important decisions on his own responsibility. He had to learn to maintain a dialogue with his priests. He had to learn serenity, lest he do things that would make the situation worse. He had to learn boldness, in order to be able to confront and denounce the powerful. He had to learn to give the people hope, and to receive from them their suffering, their faith, and their commitment. Within himself, he had to learn his faith in the God of the poor, who was also the God greater than all else, greater than his earlier ideas of God, and greater than the church itself, which was gradually becoming his cross. He had to learn that there is nothing more important than the Reign of God—that there was nothing more important than life, hope, love, and a communion of sisters and brothers. He had to learn that the church's place is among the suffering poor. The church must be immersed in the reality of the crucified peoples. The church must become a genuine Servant of Yahweh, as he would later say. Thus Archbishop Romero had to learn not only to give, but to receive light and salvation from these crucified peoples. And he learned all these things.

I never spoke of these matters with Archbishop Romero. But I suppose that his apprenticeship, like that of Jesus, must have been a painful one. I believe that Archbishop Romero wrestled with God as Jacob did, and lived out in the desert, like Jesus. More than once he must have asked God to let some chalice pass, and must have stood before God with the groans and lamentations of the true priest of the Letter to the Hebrews.

But I also could see that his conversion was a source of an immense peace, an immense freedom, and an immense joy. Here was someone who was rather shy by nature, in poor health so that he had always been forced to take an occasional physical and psychological rest cure, and who was now suddenly transformed into a strong person. I do not recall his having been ill at all during these years, or that he had to go anywhere for a psychological rest. His work load had increased immeasurably, but he fled none of the countless demands of his new task. He refused no request. On the contrary, he always seemed excited by new things to do, new projects, new topics for his pastoral letters. Sister Teresa, now deceased, his guardian angel in the little hospital, would see his light on in the late hours of the night and beg him not to work so hard. Archbishop Romero would answer simply that he had not yet said his rosary. It was no use trying to persuade him to slow down. Archbishop Romero had suddenly become an indefatigable laborer, and his store of energy was the astonishment of one and all.

I believe that the gospel he rediscovered in those days was not only a demand made on him, but a source of his strength, as well. Never did I hear him bewail his sufferings or complain about the amount of work he had to do. As he walked with the people in the strength of the gospel, and as the people walked with him, he performed his archiepiscopal ministry admirably to the end—which came at the altar of his chapel in the little hospital.

And he performed it joyfully. Of all the people I have ever known, Archbishop Romero is the one who best exemplifies Karl Rahner's words of genius: "The gospel is a light burden in the sense that the more one bears it, the more one is borne by it."

Conversion placed a terrible burden on Archbishop Romero's shoulders, but lo and behold, the burden became light, and gave him courage, energy, freedom, and joy.

VI

Three months after his appointment, Archbishop Romero had become a different bishop. He had changed. Repression and terror raged on all sides. In May 1977 the situation of the country actually took a turn for the worse, and persecution of the church became institutionalized. On May 1 a young Jesuit was arrested, then a week later turned over to his provincial and Archbishop Romero. The archbishop gave him a cup of coffee and refused to sign a statement that he had not been mistreated. On May 11 Father Alfonso Navarro was murdered. Again there was a huge Mass, and a major homily by Archbishop Romero. The situation in the country, he said, was like a caravan lost in the desert, and a bedouin would come along and show the travelers the right way and they would put him to death. On May 19 the army went to Aguilares, expelled the three remaining Jesuits, desecrated the church and sacristy, and declared a state of emergency. No one might enter Aguilares, not even the apostolic nuncio. And many *campesinos* were killed.

Repression and persecution increased rapidly, but Archbishop Romero already had a very clear notion of what he was to do. His attitude was one of determination, and his priests were remarkably receptive to his leadership. All this stood him in good stead on June 19.

After a month of the state of emergency, the army simply drove the people out of Aguilares. Archbishop Romero decided to go there at the first opportunity, denounce the atrocities that had been committed, and try to inspire a threatened, terrorized people with hope. A good many of us went along with him. It was a day I shall never forget.

The opening words of his homily are etched forever in my memory. "I have the job of picking up the trampled, the corpses, and all that persecution of the church dumps along the road on its way through." I thought: What a new, what a tragic, and what a perfect definition of the episcopal ministry! Only years later would Archbishop Romero reduce his celebrated "ministry of accompaniment" to theoretical expression. This was the day he formulated it in its maximal concretion, as he also did toward the end of his life, in February 1980, when a journalist asked him what the church would do if a war broke out. He answered that he would stand his ground "even if the only thing I could do was collect dead bodies and grant absolution to the dying." In these words, the option for the poor, so resoundingly demanded at Puebla, received profound, radical expression, and was shown to be worlds apart from anything like casual, empty chatter. And I thought: It's true, then. Archbishop Romero has made an option for his suffering people.

In his homily that day he also uttered a prophetic denunciation of those who "have transformed a people into a prison and a torture chamber." As well as I can remember, this was the first of so many homilies that, by their content, their courage, and the power of their expression showed the world that Archbishop Romero was a prophet in the strict, most authentic sense. Years later, in 1980, a scripture scholar, José Luis Sicre, an expert on the Old Testament prophets, told me: "I doubt that there have been more than a dozen authentic prophets, in the biblical sense, in the course of history—Amos, Isaiah, and so on. One of them is Oscar Romero."

Archbishop Romero's homily also provided a good example of his habit of thanking everyone who helped him and who rendered service to the church. He thanked the Jesuits for the work of Rutilio Grande and his fellow priests. And he thanked the Oblates of the Sacred Heart—the sisters who had had the courage to take charge of the parish of Aguilares when no priest dared work there any longer.

I also recall—and for me, this was the most striking thing in his homily—the great love Archbishop Romero showed for those *campesinos* of Aguilares, those suffering, terrified people, who had experienced such awful things over the previous month. How could they be helped to maintain their hope? How could they be given back at least their dignity in suffering? How could they be told that they were the most important thing to God and the church? Archbishop Romero put it this way: "You are the image of the divine victim 'pierced for our offenses,' of whom the first reading speaks to us this morning." You are Christ today, suffering in history, he told them. And in another homily, given toward the end of 1979, which I also remember very well, again speaking of the Servant of Yahweh, Archbishop Romero said that our liberator, Jesus Christ, so "identified with the people that scripture scholars do not know whether the Servant of Yahweh in Isaiah is the suffering people or Christ come to redeem us." To tell afflicted *campesinos* that they are Christ today in history, and to tell them that sincerely, is the most radical way a Christian has of restoring to them at least their dignity, and of helping them maintain their hope.

At Aguilares, Archbishop Romero went on: "We suffer with those who have suffered so much. . . . We suffer with the lost — those who have had to run away and who do not know what is happening to their families. . . . We are with those who are being tortured. . . ." I am with you, Archbishop Romero told the people, and they knew he was telling the truth. This miracle does not happen every day. But it happened here. The *campesinos* of Aguilares came into Archbishop Romero's heart and stayed there forever. And Archbishop Romero entered the hearts of all poor, simple, and suffering Salvadorans, and he is there today.

Archbishop Romero genuinely loved his people. He *only* loved them. He did not do as others, who, while loving the people, seek also their own personal, partisan, church interests. Archbishop Romero's love for his people caused him to relativize all else beside. As a result he could risk all that was not love for his people, even the institutional element in the church, even his own life. This is what has made Archbishop Romero such a source of hope, courage, and comfort for all suffering Salvadorans.

After Mass we held a procession of the Blessed Sacrament. We processed out into the little square in front of the church to make reparation for the soldiers' desecration of the sacramental Body of Christ and the living Body of Christ, the murdered *campesinos*. Across the square, in front of the town hall, were armed troops, standing there watching us, sullen, arrogant, and unfriendly. As the procession drew near the town hall we stopped. We were uneasy. In fact, we were afraid. We had no idea what might happen. And we all instinctively turned around and looked at Archbishop Romero, who was bringing up the rear, holding the monstrance. *"Adelante* (Forward!)," said Archbishop Romero. And we went right ahead. The procession ended without incident. From that moment forward, Archbishop Romero was the symbolic leader of El Salvador. He made no such claim. He had sought no such thing. But this is the way it was. From now on, Archbishop Romero led us, marching at our head. He had been transformed into the central reference point for the church and for the country. Nothing of any importance occurred in our country over the next three years without our all turning to Archbishop Romero for guidance and direction, for leadership.

As I have said, that day was very important for me personally. I saw Archbishop Romero transformed into a giant, while I was like a dwarf. I have already recounted how I tried to cooperate with him in every way, from the very start, placing my knowledge and my time at his service. What else could I have done in such tragic moments, with a recently appointed archbishop overwhelmed with his new responsibility and asking for help with such humility? But I have to confess that in those first weeks I thought that it was I who was helping him, and he who profited — that my theological ideas were surely more useful to him than his could ever be to me. And I doubt that I was the only one to feel that way. It was not a matter of trying to manipulate him. We only wanted to help him. Besides, Archbishop Romero very promptly demonstrated his evangelical autonomy. But the fact remained that our job was to help Archbishop Romero. Then came that day at Aguilares, with the Mass and procession, and I began to see things in a very different light. It was not I who was helping Archbishop Romero, but he who was helping me. It was not I who would be teaching him, but he who was teaching us. Archbishop Romero had already outdistanced us along the pathway of our pilgrimage — not by virtue of his formal authority as our archbishop, but on the strength of his evangelical and Salvadoran behavior. I hope that this does not sound like false humility. Archbishop Romero asked us to help him in a thousand ways. He expected us to help him. And we did. I think that we were very helpful to him. But when it came to basics, he had outstripped us. No longer was he the freshly appointed, nervous, overwhelmed archbishop. Now he was the trail-blazer, marching at our head, and in the most fundamental matters.

And I recall the impact Archbishop Romero had on my theology that day. His celebration of the eucharist at Aguilares was a revelation to me. Besides being the eucharist, it was also — although neither he nor I thought of it in this way at the time — a lesson in theology. Not that anything was added to the traditional themes of the eucharist: thanksgiving, the word, the sacrifice, the presence of Christ, the offering, the community, and so on. And of course all of these theological themes were extremely familiar to me in their theoretical form. But Archbishop Romero developed them *in actu,* with a truth and creativity that taught me more about the eucharist than I had learned in all my long years of study. From that moment on, Archbishop Romero became a source of inspiration to me even in the area of theology, as I explained in my address (see below, pp. 168–88) on the occasion of the posthumous conferral on him of the honorary doctorate in theology by the University of Central America.

In all sincerity, and with all gratitude, I must acknowledge that Archbishop Romero's life, work, and word — a word spoken from deep within that life and that work — have been my theological light and inspiration. I do not think that, without Archbishop Romero, I could ever have achieved a satisfactory theological formulation of things as basic as the mystery of God, the church of the poor, hope, martyrdom, Christian fellowship, the essence of the gospel as good news, or even of Jesus Christ, whose three years of life and mission, cross and resurrection, have now been illuminated for me by Archbishop Romero's three years as archbishop. Archbishop Romero also made me realize the importance of using current reality as a theological argument. I shall spare the reader any lengthy theoretical discussion here, and simply observe that while, as every theologian knows, in order to do theology one must use Scripture, tradition, and the magisterium, I began to realize that one must also use reality to explain theological content. What is hope? What is martyrdom? What is a bishop? What is prophecy? Archbishop

Romero and others—as part of the reality around me—have shed light on these things for me.

I spoke with Archbishop Romero a number of times on theological matters, and he showed great interest in our discussions. He wanted to see theology function in the service of the church's mission. He also had a deep appreciation of theology as something valuable in itself, apart from any use that might be made of it for an ulterior end. Very early in the three years of his archiepiscopal ministry he explained to me that, while of course the church was engaged in a pastoral reaction to the persecution and martyrdom it was undergoing, a theological reflection would be necessary as well. He asked me to write about this, and I did. My research turned up very little existing theology on persecution and martyrdom of the kind that were occurring in El Salvador, and I had to begin to build my theological argumentation from a point of departure in reality. Archbishop Romero also asked me to reflect on the church and its mission, and on evangelization, especially as the latter is presented in Paul VI's *Evangelii Nuntiandi,* on which I based a three-day workshop for priests. A number of us Salvadoran theologians, social analysts, and pastoral ministers now began to address the urgent problems of our land—the popular organizations, the violence all around, and the mission of the church in the presence of these concrete realities. I remember the many long meetings we held with Archbishop Romero—the discussions, the explanations he asked for, the drafting and redrafting of what we proposed to publish, and his final decision. Before he went to Puebla he called me to see him three times, to talk over the most important theological points to be taken up by the bishops there. I recall particularly well that he wondered why some liberation theologians criticized the social teaching of the church. I explained this to him, identifying the various theoretical problems posed by the social teaching of the church and its pastoral application. But what struck me is how calmly he asked about this—simply from a need to understand, without feeling obliged as an archbishop to defend every detail of the social teaching of the church as a matter of faith, and yet without the slightest concern merely to keep up with the latest fashion in theology. He spoke completely naturally about these problems.

We talked a great deal about theology, then. What Archbishop Romero never knew, or what in his humility never occurred to him, was that, with his questions, his theological problems, and above all with his word and his life, he helped me a great deal in my own practice of theology. It may be that we helped him to conceptualize theological problems (and it seems to me that, as far as conceptualization is concerned, Archbishop Romero never got much beyond the theological level of Vatican II, although the theological content of his words and actions was biblical and historical as well, and perfectly adequate to the intentions of the theology of liberation). But he helped us, too, and more radically than we helped him. His theological assistance to us was not on the level of technical conceptualization, but on a much more important one: that of inspiration and light to see and better deal with the fundamental theological realities—God as seen from this world, and this world as seen from the standpoint of God. As Gustavo Gutiérrez puts it, the basic problem of liberation theology is how to tell the poor of this world that God loves them. And this is the problem on which Archbishop Romero was able to shed so much light.

The reason I have devoted so much space to detailing the impact that Archbishop Romero had on all of us, especially on me, is not that I am in any way concerned about biographical data for their own sake, but that I want to lay to rest for good and all the tired old allegation that Archbishop Romero was "manipulated" by us. I must sincerely say that if there was any manipulation, Archbishop Romero manipulated us more than we manipulated him. Archbishop Romero gave us more than we gave him. That is my conviction, and my hope.

VII

Between the day we met at Aguilares and the day he died, I spoke with Archbishop Romero time and again, at the chancery, in the little hospital, or in the house where we Jesuits live. He paid us fairly frequent visits. We could see that he was at ease at our house. I remember how, before taking his leave, he always stopped into the kitchen to thank our cook, which gave her a great deal of pleasure.

I shall not attempt to detail all of the things that impressed me in the remaining nearly three years of Archbishop Romero's ministry. Many of them are familiar to all: his Sunday homilies at the cathedral, his constant visits to the base communities, his pastoral letters, his openness to dialogue with one and all, even persons belonging to the oligarchy and the armed forces, who would sometimes go to see him under cover of night, like Nicodemus in St. John's Gospel, to ask his help with some personal problem. His national and international prestige grew by leaps and bounds. So did the hostility of the oligarchy, the army, the government, and his fellow bishops, until the alarm sounded in the offices of the North American government itself.

Were I to attempt to sum up in a single word the many, many aspects of Archbishop Romero's activity during these years, I should have to say that what impressed me most was his thoroughgoing *consistency* in following his chosen path—his *fidelity* to that path. The basic principle of this consistency was his option for the poor. For Archbishop Romero this was a theological principle in the strictest sense, since he had made God the prototype of all his activity. It was an ecclesiological principle, as well, since he had erected this option into the criterion of all of the activity of his church. And it was a prudential principle for him, since he had to see to it that the option for the poor assumed various concretions in function of the changing historical situation of our country. The heart and soul of this principle was the correlation between God and the poor, between the church and the poor.

It is not difficult to parrot the principle that the church exists for the sake of the Reign of God, that it should make an option for the poor—even that the poor are our evangelizers, and so on. But how difficult it is to practice this basic principle of hope and ecclesiology! And Archbishop Romero practiced it to the end. There cannot be the slightest doubt that he proclaimed the good news to the poor and defended them to the end. But since this is such a rare phenomenon—since he did so in such an exceptional, radical way—one is also struck by the clear-sightedness with which he expounded the option for the poor, the way he theorized it, and how he erected it to a criterion of action. It became the practical principle of all his activity, whatever the latter might happen to be. To use one of his own crisp, finely chiseled phrases: "The natural partner for the church's dialogue is the people, not the government." With these words— and their implementation in practice—he reduced centuries of Christendom, along with the ever-recurrent intentions of a neo-Christendom, to dust. The much desired, long sought after goal of harmony between the church and the powers of this world— the state, the armed forces, economic powers, political powers— simply did not figure among Archbishop Romero's goals. In practice this ideal could not have been attained in any case, of course, since these powers were constantly and viciously on the attack against the church. But this is not the point. Archbishop Romero opposed this ideal on principle. He opposed it simply because the world of power is not the world of the church. What was really to be desired and striven for was the church's harmony with, and compenetration with, the poor. Or in another lapidary expression of his: "The church will judge a given political project on the basis of whether or not it does the people any good." Here again was the novelty of Archbishop Romero. He was unwilling to judge political projects a priori, on the criterion of an ideology, as the church usually does, with its weakness for Christian Democratic ideologies and its mistrust of anything like socialism; and least of all was he willing to judge them according to whether they favor, flatter, or privilege the institutional church. His criterion was the good of the people, period—the impoverished masses. That criterion was no more and no less than the concrete application in El Salvador of the first and last scriptural criterion of the activity of God, of Jesus, and of the human being par excellence: mercy.

If we see a suffering people, a people lying in the ditch by the side of the road, what must we do—with absolute urgency, over and above all other considerations? Must we not lift those people from their prostration, heal their wounds, and stay by their side until they are completely well? Next, Archbishop Romero emphasized, since the victim in the ditch is a whole people, the remedy, the healing, must be structural. Thus his pastoral letters analyzed the structural roots of our ills, and studied the possible paths to justice, the roads leading to liberation from those ills. Archbishop Romero was a visionary here.

Such was Archbishop Romero's compassion for the poor. All of his activity was steeped in this compassion, this mercy. In fact, his relationship with the poor went far beyond works of mercy. He fairly rushed to the poor, in order to receive from them, to learn from them, and to enable them to impart to him the good news. I recall how surprised I was when I learned that, in the course of his work on the document he intended to present to the Puebla Conference, a document on the condition of the archdiocese, he sent out a questionnaire to the parishes and base communities—some of whose members probably could neither read nor write—asking them what they thought of the country and the church, what they thought was the greatest sin, who Jesus Christ was for them, and what they thought of the bishops conference, the apostolic nuncio, and the archbishop himself. I was surprised (sadly enough, since this ought to be a bishop's normal *modus operandi*) that Archbishop Romero would ask the people of God their opinion. But I was even more surprised when he took their answers seriously. I was part of the team that compiled and analyzed them, and I remember this very well. This meant that Archbishop Romero was really open to others— open to being helped and taught by the poor. He followed the same procedure in composing his pastoral letters.

Archbishop Romero believed in his people. You could see how proud he was of them. Here was the church of the poor. "You! A church so filled with life! A church so filled with the Holy Spirit!" he would tell them. He could not conceal the joy he had in this church composed of the poor, the *campesinos*, the outcasts. At the peak of their repression and persecution, he uttered the following words, which show what he thought of his church of the poor:

If they ever take our radio [which had already been jammed and bombed], suspend our newspaper, silence us, put to death all of us priests, bishop included, and you are left alone—a people without priests—then each of you will have to be God's microphone. Each of you will have to be a messenger, a prophet. The church will always exist as long as even one baptized person is left alive!

The impact of words like these on the people was like a jolt of electric current. Archbishop Romero trusted his people. He was proud of them. He loved them. And he let himself be loved by them — something seemingly so easy, but actually very difficult. "I just love it when the people in those little villages, with their kids and all, run up and crowd around." Some of these poor once came to the archiepiscopal chancery with chicks for Archbishop Romero. I was told — and I suppose it really happened — that they once brought him a cow, causing no little consternation and commotion at the curia. They wrote him unpretentious, informal letters about their personal problems, and Archbishop Romero answered them. They sent him alms, out of their poverty: a peso, a few centavos. When his friends were murdered his innards wrenched with pain. He would say, "I love their names — Felipe de Jesús Chacón, Polín [as we called Apolinario]. . . . I just broke down and cried when I heard." His people filled his heart. He let himself be loved, and this is the most radical way to span distances and burst boundaries, which always exist between those of high and low estate.

He judged political and social forces from the viewpoint of the poor. He saw that the forces of the right (the government, the oligarchy, the army and the security forces, the judiciary, most of the media, and the U.S. Embassy) oppressed the poor, and he denounced them all, exposed them, and called for their radical conversion. All this is well known, and I need not belabor it. But I do want to recall Archbishop Romero's attitude toward the left, which is much less well understood. He defended, supported, and rejoiced in the rise of the popular organizations, which he went so far as to call "signs of the times" in the sense in which Jesus used the expression (Matt. 16:3). He surely saw far more representative popular reality in them than in their adversaries. "I don't call them the forces of the left," he declared; "I call them the forces of the people." Since he was responsible for pastoral ministry in his diocese, he insisted on a ministry of accompaniment, lest these organizations remain merely popular, and not imbued with the spirit of the gospel.

But he criticized them, as well, and certainly more forcefully and analytically than the church has done since then. He criticized them, however, not because they were of the left — the sole, simplistic objection of the other bishops, as if being on the left were the worst imaginable evil—but precisely because (if I may be permitted an expression that they would certainly find offensive) some of their attitudes were actually antipopular. He criticized their internal divisions, their eagerness for hegemony over other leftist organizations, and their chauvinism, as if only a popular organization could ever render service to the people. And of course he condemned certain terrorist activities and certain tendencies to manipulate popular piety in the interests of the organization. Archbishop Romero saw that none of this favored the poor. Archbishop Romero has been called uncritical and naive when it came to the people's organizations. Nothing could be further from the truth. Not only was he critical of them, he actually warned them of the danger of transforming themselves into an idol—the most serious warning that a religion can conceivably issue—just as he forthrightly denounced the idolatry of capitalism and the national security doctrine. In fact, under the first junta (October 15, 1979, to January 2, 1980) he was actually accused by some of our communities and priests of having given his blessing to the new rightist government! I recall a heated discussion between Rogelio Ponseele, a priest now serving in Morazán, and Archbishop Romero on this point in a clergy meeting. The discussion was a heated one, as I say, but Archbishop Romero stood his ground. Afterwards, Rogelio wept when Archbishop Romero was murdered, and wrote of him: "He was a unique occurrence in the history of the church. He is a miracle."

My point is that, contrary to the notions entertained by certain misinformed persons and groups, Archbishop Romero criticized the people's organizations. He did so, of course, only because their errors were harmful to the people. And the purpose of his criticism was to get the popular organizations back on track, back serving the people. Whether he was supporting the people's organizations or criticizing them, his operative criterion was that of the good of the poor, the Reign of God. It was this criterion that made him want to become more familiar with the organizations, and this was at the basis of his invitations to them to attend our clergy meetings and present their views— something the other bishops could not imagine doing, since their

approach was simply to condemn the organizations out of hand
for being on the left. Archbishop Romero wanted to inspire
them to unite, to join forces. When he learned that the popular
organizations had adopted a common platform, great was his
joy. He saw this as an important step in terms of the good of
the poor.

Today Archbishop Rivera tells of a conversation he had with
Joaquín Villalobos—one of the five *comandantes* of the FMLN,
the Farabundo Marti National Liberation Front—years after
Archbishop Romero's death. Villalobos had mentioned Archbishop Romero's name several times in the course of the discussion, and finally told Archbishop Rivera: "If Romero were
alive today he would really 'let us have it.' But he would also
understand us." Personally I think Villalobos was correct. I think
Archbishop Romero would denounce many of the things the
FMLN does. He certainly would condemn its murder of civilians.
But I think he would understand them—not as a politico-military movement, but as an expression (tragic or hopeful, de-
pending on where your sympathies lie) of the desire to do away
with the sufferings of the poor, the ongoing injustice, and institutionalized lying of which the poor are the victims. He would
ask them to keep up these ideals, and he would criticize their
errors. And most of all he would ask them—as he always asked
everyone—to keep their eyes fixed on the good of the whole
people.

Archbishop Romero's behavior was guided by his option for
the poor, then. This had many consequences. Now the church
was credible, religion was accepted or at least respected, and
Salvadorans, especially the poor, were given heart and hope.
But the effect I want to emphasize is that, with Archbishop
Romero, the church—and the faith—became Salvadoran and
Christian. The more the faith is lived in El Salvador in a Christian way, the more Salvadoran it becomes. And the more our
Salvadoran reality is lived to the hilt, the more Christian our
faith becomes. Faith and our Salvadoran reality, church and
country, are no longer mutually diluting quantities. Now they
reinforce each other.

Archbishop Romero expressed this convergence in his life as
in his death. And he also spoke these most perceptive words,

which sent chills up people's spines when they were pronounced, and sends chills up their spines today:

> I rejoice, brothers and sisters, that our church is persecuted precisely for its preferential option for the poor, and for seeking to become incarnate in the interests of the poor.... How sad it would be, in a country where such horrible murders are being committed, if there were no priests among the victims! A murdered priest is a testimonial of a church incarnate in the problems of the people.... The church suffers the lot of the poor—persecution. It is the glory of our church to have mixed its blood—the blood of its priests, catechists, and communities—with the massacres of the people, and ever to have borne the mark of persecution.... A church that suffers no persecution, but enjoys the privileges and support of the powers of this world—that church has good reason to be afraid! But that church is not the true church of Jesus Christ.

The goal for which Archbishop Romero strove was a Christian Salvadoran, or Salvadoran Christian, church. And he reached that goal. The price the church had to pay was great: enrollment in the ranks of the victims of the Salvadoran bloodletting. But the church was also richly rewarded: now the Salvadoran poor have the knowledge and experience that they are truly the church of Jesus Christ. After a talk I once gave on this subject at a theological congress, an African priest commented to me that the thing Archbishop Romero's words just cited made him think most about was that no priests in his country had "been killed so far." His remark made me shiver, but I think he was saying something very important. I think he was saying that the Christian church will not become African in his country until it shares the concrete sufferings and hopes of his people.

What Archbishop Romero achieved by practicing what he preached was a Salvadoran church, and therefore a church of the people. If he were alive today, I think it would give him a great deal of pain to hear the expression "popular church" used—by those outside that church—in the sense of a bad church, a suspect church. Archbishop Romero would continue to criticize the shortcomings of the poor in the church. But, he would wonder, how can a genuinely Salvadoran church of Jesus be anything but a church of the people?

VIII

The last time I saw Archbishop Romero alive was on my return from a meeting of bishops, theologians, and pastoral ministers in São Paulo, Brazil, in February 1980. I seem to recall he had been invited to the meeting himself, but had preferred not to leave the country in the current circumstances, which were growing more alarming by the day. Then, some two weeks before his assassination, he came to the Jesuit house, and I conveyed to him the greetings that had been sent him by a number of parties in Brazil, especially an expression of support from Bishop Pedro Casaldáliga, whom I had met there for the first time. Dom Pedro also wrote Archbishop Romero a letter, and it arrived in time for him to read it. His response would bear the date of March 24, and would be found among his effects: it had been typed, but not signed. Archbishop Romero must have dictated it only a few hours before his death. A month later Archbishop Rivera had the thoughtfulness to send it to Dom Pedro, who prizes it as a genuine relic. As it is one of Archbishop Romero's last letters—the last one, in fact, that he ever wrote—I shall reproduce it here verbatim.

San Salvador, March 24, 1980

His Excellency
Bishop Pedro Casaldáliga
São Félix, Brazil

Dear Brother in the Episcopate:

It is with deep affection that I thank you for your brotherly message of regret over the destruction of our radio station. Your warm support is a great inspiration to us as we strive to keep on with our mission of expressing the hopes and the anguish of the poor, in a spirit of joy at being accorded the privilege of running the same risks as they, as Jesus did by identifying with the causes of the dispossessed.

In the light of faith, and in intimate union of affection, prayer, and the triumph of the resurrection,

I remain,
Oscar A. Romero
Archbishop

"Joy at being accorded the privilege of running the same risks as they, as Jesus did by identifying with the causes of the dispossessed." This is a perfect description of what Archbishop Romero did, and quite consciously, during the last months of his life. I have cited the consistency of his behavior. Now let me speak of his fidelity in the face of so many attacks and threats on his person and his life. Verbal assaults began very early. "Monseñor Romero Sells His Soul to Satan," ran the headline of a little paper published by the ultra-right, a paper which did not last very long after that. Physical threats on his life came later. A few weeks before his death, dozens of sticks of unexploded dynamite were found in a church in which he had celebrated Mass.

Archbishop Romero was aware that his life was in danger, but he remained faithful to his convictions. He refused to run away, he made no deals, and far from softening his denunciations, he redoubled them. In fact, he refused the secret service protection offered him by the president of the republic, his public response, in a homily, being: "I hereby inform the president that, rather than my own security, what I should like to have is security and tranquility for 108 families and their 'disappeared.' . . . A shepherd seeks no security as long as the flock is threatened."

It was not long before Archbishop Romero realized that he was threatened with a violent death. Death was coming out of the woodwork in El Salvador; why should the victims' leader be spared? In the last retreat he ever made, the one we have already mentioned, he jotted down what he had said to his director, Father Azcue, and what the latter had replied:

> My other fear is for my life. It is not easy to accept a violent death, which is very possible in these circumstances, and the apostolic nuncio to Costa Rica warned me of imminent danger just this week. You have encouraged me, reminding me that my attitude should be to hand my life over to God regardless of the end to which that life might come; that unknown circumstances can be faced with God's grace; that God assisted the martyrs, and that if it comes to this I shall feel God very close as I draw my last breath; but that more valiant than surrender in death is the surrender of one's whole life — a life lived for God.

Personally I never heard Archbishop Romero speak of these things. In any event, he kept moving ahead in the last month remaining to him, and preached valiantly. Afterwards, we learned that in mid-March he had told a journalist from Venezuela that he had often received death threats. In the situation in our country, with repression on the wax, with six priests already dead, it did occur to us that Archbishop Romero himself might be killed. But I think we tried not to believe it, such was our affection for him and the magnitude of the prospective atrocity. At any rate we never spoke of it. On March 23 we heard his last Sunday homily and his last public words:

> In the name of God, then, and in the name of this suffering people, whose screams and cries mount to heaven, and daily grow louder, I beg you, I entreat you, I order you in the name of God: Stop the repression!

I do not know whether these words were his death sentence or not. I suppose it takes more than a few days to work out a professional assassination, and Archbishop Romero had only a few days to live when he said these words. But these words certainly consummated the process of truth-telling and denunciation of atrocities that objectively led to Archbishop Romero's martyrdom. I was personally moved by his words, and most concerned.

On the evening of March 24 the telephone at the Jesuit residence rang. Someone wanted to talk to one of the Fathers. I was the only one there at the time, so I took the call. It was a sister from the hospital where Archbishop Romero lived. She was beside herself, and was screaming almost hysterically. "Monseñor has been shot! He's covered with blood!" That was the only thing she said that I could understand. She was obviously in no condition to explain anything. I was not even able to learn whether Monseñor was alive or dead.

I left the house at once and hurried over to the provincial's office, practically next door. I told Father Provincial César Jerez about the phone call, and we turned on the radio. And we heard: "Monseñor Romero is dead." César Jerez and I sat in silence for a good little while. Then I went to Central American University. I shall never forget the scene. Some twenty persons — stalwart persons, persons accustomed to being attacked, persons used to bad news — were standing motionless, their faces a study in helplessness and despair. They did not speak. Yes, Archbishop Romero was dead. (Days later I learned that I was the first priest to learn the news. The nuns at the hospital had tried to call Monseñor Ricardo Urioste, a vicar general, but they had not been able to locate him. Then they called the Jesuit residence. I say this in parentheses, but it was something of a little personal consolation to me to realize that the nuns he stayed with regarded us as close to him.)

The first hours after the murder would have reminded you of the behavior of the apostles after the death of Jesus. Despair, grief, and confusion reigned. But very quickly, in fact in a much shorter time than the ten days St. Luke says the apostles sat trembling in the Upper Room, the Spirit breathed, and mightily. A huge mobilization was suddenly under way. There were Masses for Archbishop Romero, meetings, communiqués, notes, and letters. Telephone calls began coming in from all over the world. Journalists requested interviews. Delegations arrived, conveying the support of some group that loved or admired him. Like Jesus — who was also murdered and martyred — Archbishop Romero began to generate life even after his own death, in El

Salvador as elsewhere, among Christians and nonbelievers alike. I can recall nothing of the kind in my experience since the death of John XXIII. By way of one anecdote out of a thousand: a labor union in Czechoslovakia sent us a message of solidarity.

"If they kill me, I shall rise again in the Salvadoran people. I am not boasting; I say it with the greatest humility," Archbishop Romero had declared only a few days before. How quickly his words came true. His funeral on March 30 was, more than anything else, a formidable expression of that resurrection, one of the greatest I have ever seen. But it was also the largest popular demonstration in the history of El Salvador. And of course it was the most heartfelt, most sorrowful, and most affectionate demonstration El Salvador had ever seen. We all wept, and from the depths of us. Yes, there were a few Salvadorans who toasted Archbishop Romero's death with champagne. A few. But the masses of the poor wept for him as one weeps only for a mother or a father.

And as we know, on that March 30 there were new blood and new tears, at the most incredible funeral in modern history. The evening before, we had reflected that something could happen at the funeral, since the memory of the massacre at a popular demonstration on January 22 that same year was still fresh in everyone's mind. We did not speak a great deal of this, and we tried to persuade ourselves that nothing like that would actually happen. But it did. Several persons died of suffocation or gunshot wounds. Almost all of the bishops and priests stayed in the cathedral, to be with the thousands who tried to reach safety inside. We hoped we might be able to offer these defenseless persons some protection. Only Cardinal Corripio, Archbishop of Mexico City, who was the papal legate at the funeral, left, hurrying for the airport. Archbishop Romero's death had caused sorrow and confusion. His funeral caused indignation and incredulity. An Italian journalist wept. Another journalist, from a South American country, I believe, told me while we were there barricaded inside the cathedral: "I thought I'd seen everything. I was in Vietnam. But I've never seen anything like this." And as Archbishop Romero's body was buried in great haste in the cathedral, his spirit began to fly across the entire world.

Those days were days of great agitation for us, and a great

deal of work, as well. I began to write my first reflections on Archbishop Romero's life and death. I had not even had the time to go to his wake in the cathedral. It was not difficult for me to describe the events of his life and the details of his death. But I quickly realized that it was going to be very difficult indeed to describe Archbishop Romero himself. Who was he? Who is he? This is a question that goes far beyond the details of his life and death. It is the question of the totality of Archbishop Romero. It is the question that arises with the death of John XXIII or Martin Luther King. I think that it is also the question—in due proportion, of course—that arose in the minds of the first Christians: Who was this Jesus of Nazareth, after all? Who was this person who had been murdered and then raised from the dead? I soon became convinced that Archbishop Romero was a "gospel"—good news from God.

We shall have to write his biography in detail one day. We shall have to analyze, interpret, and explain his actions and his thinking. That goes without saying. But I have become convinced that the reality of Archbishop Romero cannot be communicated through analysis alone. One must have allowed oneself to be affected by the totality of his person. We see the same thing in what the gospels say of Jesus. After Archbishop Romero's funeral I began to write a long article about him (see chapter 2, below). I finished it on April 10. In it I sought to analyze his person as a believer, an archbishop, and a Salvadoran. And I generated a great deal of paper. But behind the analysis was the overall impact Archbishop Romero had on me. In those days I formulated it in this way: "Archbishop Romero believed in God." It was with that faith of his that he accomplished his infinitude of good. In that faith I discovered the root of everything else. And that faith, for me, was good news—a gospel.

I have personally verified this conviction of mine that it is impossible to communicate who Archbishop Romero is without allowing oneself to be affected by him, without comprehending him as the gospel that he so often was, especially to poor, simple people. Within days, within hours, handbills and posters carrying his picture had been printed and distributed. In no time at all, the people had composed songs and verses about him. Suddenly the people were explicitly referring to him as a shepherd, a prophet, and a martyr. But there was something that went even deeper. A number of times I have asked simple people, in so many words, who Archbishop Romero was. And the answer has come back: "Archbishop Romero told the truth, and defended us because we are poor, so they shot him." There is perceptivity in these words, and admiration. But more than anything else, there is love. In Archbishop Romero people saw someone who really loved them. And this is a piece of good news, a gospel.

During these same days I received a letter from Dom Pedro Casaldáliga, bishop of São Félix, Brazil. I had written him on my return from São Paulo, asking him to write to Archbishop Romero to encourage him in his painful situation in the church itself. In his reply, Casaldáliga wished me Easter joy — as was his wont — and sent me the poem that has become a classic on our continent, "Saint Romero of the Americas." How many times I have read it in El Salvador, and how deeply it has moved my hearers and myself! I have become convinced that Dom Pedro Casaldáliga truly understood Archbishop Romero. He wrote about him in a way that showed that he had been affected by him: he wrote about him with truth and love.

Years later, in 1985, Dom Pedro came to El Salvador and visited Archbishop Romero's tomb. In the evening, in a little ceremony we had in the Archbishop Romero Chapel at Central American University, Dom Pedro spoke to us of many things. Finally he stood as if to leave. But a nun stood up and said: "Bishop Casaldáliga, we've read your poem about Archbishop Romero so many times. Now we'd like to ask you to read it." We all rose, and Dom Pedro Casaldáliga recited his poem. The silence, the devotion, and the joy with which every one of us listened convinced me all over again that Archbishop Romero was still good news. "I started to pray again tonight," a friend told me after the service.

IX

Dom Pedro's poem ends:

> Saint Romero of the Americas,
> our shepherd and our martyr,

no one shall ever silence
your last homily.

Is this true? Archbishop Romero has surely become a universal figure. He is obviously not the only Christian, or only bishop, ever to have been murdered. But in virtue of the quality of his life and work, in virtue of the historical circumstances of his martyrdom, by virtue of his incredible funeral, he has become a universal figure. We should have to go back to Thomas à Becket, archbishop of Canterbury—in the twelfth century—to find a bishop who was murdered at the altar. And even so there is a key difference. Thomas à Becket was assassinated for defending the rights and liberties of the church. Archbishop Romero was assassinated for defending the poor of the Reign of God. José María Valverde, professor of esthetics at the University of Barcelona, has said it this way, in verses of his own:

> Dark centuries ago,
> it is told, a bishop died
> by order of a king,
> spattering the chalice with his blood
> to defend the freedom of the church
> from the secular might.
> Well enough, surely. But
> since when has it been told
> that a bishop fell at the altar
> not for the freedom of the church,
> but simply because
> he took sides with the poor—
> because he was the mouth of their thirst for
>   justice
> crying to heaven?
> When has such a thing been told?
> Perhaps not since the beginning,
> when Someone died
> the death of a subversive
> and a slave.

And indeed the martyrdom of Archbishop Romero and so many Latin American Christians bears a greater resemblance to the death of Jesus than do other martyrdoms. For a time, some disputed whether so many Christians murdered in El Salvador ought to be called martyrs. Archbishop Romero himself put the question to rest while he was still alive:

> For me they are actual martyrs, in the popular sense. I don't mean "martyr" in the canonical sense, of course, when a martyr has been proclaimed as such to the church universal by the highest authority in that church. I respect this law, and would never refer to our murdered priests as canonized martyrs. But they are martyrs in the basic sense of the word. They have preached precisely immersion in poverty. They are genuine human beings, who have gone to the limit of danger, where the UGB [the White Warriors, a death squad] lurks, where someone can "finger" you for death and you die. This is how Christ died.

Inevitably, Archbishop Romero's death has raised the question of martyrdom in El Salvador and Latin America today. If Archbishop Romero is not a Christian martyr, who in the world is? The poor have no doubt that he is. Canonists may still have doubt. But Archbishop Romero died to defend the faith; he knew that what he was doing could cause his death, and so forth. Then how can there be any doubt? Karl Rahner, in a theological reflection on martyrdom he wrote just before his own death, called for a broadening of the traditional notion of martyrdom. "Why would not Monseñor Romero, for example, be a martyr?" he wrote. "After all, he fell in the struggle for justice in society, fell in a struggle he waged from his deepest Christian convictions." I like to interpret these words of Rahner as the grateful encomium of a great theologian on a great bishop.

The figure of Archbishop Romero as a martyr has loomed larger with the passing years. There has also been the attempt to destroy this image. But it is easy to understand why such an image should prevail. The popular songs, the books about Archbishop Romero, the handbills with his picture on them, are countless. People make pilgrimages to his tomb to pray to him, to ask him for favors, to thank him. And in all of this, a heartfelt love of the poor is expressed, and a heartfelt love of all who would continue his work. People at base community meetings constantly quote his words, and this with the evident conviction that they are speaking of someone ultimate, someone sacred. We even find a linguistic phenomenon reminiscent of the sudden New Testament reservation of the title, "Lord," to Jesus Christ alone, so that there was no need to specify "Lord Jesus": in El Salvador, "Monseñor" (literally, "My Lord," or "My Lord Bishop") simply means Archbishop Romero. The people have already made him a saint.

Throughout Latin America, then, as in so many other parts of the world, Archbishop Romero is admired and loved. Persons who never saw him find in him great strength for their faith as believers, and the strength to live their dignity as human beings. Countless solidarity committees, and so many pastoral publications, bear his name. Innumerable books and articles cite him. Plays have been written about him, as well as a little opera, and even a commercial film has been made about him. March 24 is observed as a holy day in many places. El Salvador is known today for two things, the world over: the war that is tearing it limb from limb, and Archbishop Romero. A passenger on an plane was asked, "Where are you headed?" The answer was, "El Salvador." "Ah," said the questioner, "the land of Archbishop Romero." One could relate countless similar anecdotes.

I happened to be travelling frequently in Latin America, Europe, the United States, and Canada in those days. Wherever I went, I was asked to speak about Archbishop Romero. The only time I have ever been in Asia—where my intention had been to keep my eyes open and my mouth closed—I was also asked to speak about Archbishop Romero. In Tokyo, in New Delhi, and in so many other places, I have been struck by how much Archbishop Romero means to Christians, Marxists, Buddhists, and Hindus. "I have some bad news for you," a European told me one day (a Frenchman, as I recall). "Archbishop Romero does not belong just to Salvadorans any more. He belongs to the world now."

Archbishop Romero has touched something very profound in the hearts of human beings and believers. I think he offers all of us a pathway of humanization. He has helped all of us to know a little better what we are and what we ought to be. And to all of us he has offered the reality of Jesus, and God, that all may become believers and human beings. Dom Pedro Casaldáliga has summed it up so well: "The history of the church in Latin America is divided into two parts: before and after Archbishop Romero."

All of this is perfectly clear to me. But to my surprise and sorrow, a campaign has been mounted to belittle and silence this heroic figure. Archbishop Romero was surely a good man, we hear it said, but not a very prudent or intelligent one. He was actually a weak, impressionable person; and radical groups, among them the Jesuits, latched on to him and steered him along the path of their particular interests. I recall my stupor and indignation when I was told in Caracas in 1982 that the provincial of a certain religious order had heard in Rome that Archbishop Romero had become a product of manipulation by the Jesuits. I think the "manipulation theory" has been running out of steam. At least it is no longer officially propagated since Pope John Paul II's visit to El Salvador in 1983. Altogether unexpectedly, by completely personal choice, the pope interrupted his planned itinerary and went to the Cathedral of San Salvador. On his knees he prayed at Archbishop Romero's tomb, then praised him as a "zealous shepherd, inspired by the love of God and service to his brethren to offer up his very life, suffering a violent death while celebrating the sacrifice of forgiveness and reconciliation." I have heard that the holy father regards Archbishop Romero as a genuine martyr.

Still, it will not be superfluous to devote a few lines here to an analysis of what lurks behind the oft-repeated manipulation theory. To me it is clear that Archbishop Romero was subjected to many pressures. It could not have been otherwise. The government, the oligarchy, the Vatican, and the Salvadoran Bishops Conference all pressured him. The most alert elements among the clergy, and the popular organizations, also sought to influence him. In fact, among the ten points Archbishop Romero proposed to analyze about himself in the course of his last retreat was the following: "I am afraid of ideological and political pressure. I am very vulnerable when it comes to being influenced. I may very well be under people's influence."

That Archbishop Romero was under pressure, then, and vulnerable to that pressure, is one thing, and something he recognized himself. But that his life and work are to be explained purely in terms of outside manipulation is something else again — an unwarranted conclusion, and a matter of wishful thinking. The pressure from the right was stronger. First came the cajolery, then the threats. But Archbishop Romero did not yield to this pressure. There was also real pressure from the left at times, and I think the better-advised clergy did attempt to move Archbishop Romero more toward their line of thought and action — which, for that matter, would seem to be legitimate enough. Then why not accept the obvious explanation for Archbishop Romero's behavior — that he found one line so much more evangelical than the other? I think that, *through* the pressures of the left, Archbishop Romero found the more evangelical line. But what moved him to implement this line rather than the other was not these pressures, but the intrinsic truth he was discovering, as I have tried to explain in discussing his conversion. Pressure from the left may have been one important *occasion,* among others, for his change. But they were not the *cause* of his conversion, or at the very least they were not the basic cause.

Further, I think that, whatever may have been the pressures from the left in the beginning, Archbishop Romero very quickly acquired and manifested an identity of his own. What he did June 19, 1977, at Aguilares can in no way, shape, or form be explained in terms of remote control on the part of others. It was he, Archbishop Romero, who did that. As I have said, from that day forward we felt that he was out ahead of us — that it was not he who was following in our footsteps, but we who were following in his.

This is not to deny that, over the course of three years, Archbishop Romero often felt pressure from both sides. So many things happened, so many decisions had to be made. It would be an illusion to think that Archbishop Romero acted as if he were living in some sort of isolation chamber. Nor does it seem strange to me that, from time to time, he should unburden himself and say he felt pressured. I suppose he did so privately sometimes, and it seems to me normal that he should. But he did so publicly, as well, for example in the discussion with Rogelio Ponseele that I have already mentioned: he protested that the left was pressuring him. That Archbishop Romero should live under pressure, then, seems to me altogether to be expected. That he actually thought of himself as impressionable by temperament is certainly a fact. But to wish to conclude from this that his life and work were the product of pressure seems to me to be both logically fallacious and factually untrue. Archbishop Romero acknowledged that he was impressionable, and he did so during a spiritual retreat, traditionally a time for an honest analysis of one's limitations and problems. But—although in his humility he did not admit this to himself—he was also by nature enterprising, intelligent, courageous, and altogether a determined follower of the will of God. The texture of everyone's life—even that of the saints—includes all of the data of one's character, and these data make their contribution to all of the immanent and transient activities through which one may come to be a human being and even a saint. But to seek to explain the whole of a person's life and work solely in function of one aspect of his or her personality—especially if the analysis of that personality is faulty—is disastrous. It is as if we were to say that St. Ignatius Loyola must not have experienced divine grace because he was of a voluntaristic, stubborn, and tenacious character; or as if we were to say that St. Teresa of Avila's experience of God was a delusion because she seems to have been somewhat emotionally unbalanced.

Whatever be the case with Archbishop Romero's character, then, the correct procedure will be to analyze how he reacted, with that concrete character, in the decisions he had to make in real life, and why he made these decisions. To my knowledge, whenever he had important decisions to make he asked for advice. It took him an infinitude of meetings, polls of the common people, rough drafts, and months of work to finalize his pastoral letters. Throughout the whole process, he constantly asked questions, made suggestions, and raised difficulties. This was how he proceeded. He would pray at length, then finally make his decision. In preparing his homilies, he would review the most important events of the week, and ask advice when he thought he simply had to take a prophetic, forthright, and therefore provocative position on anything. I have Sister Teresa's word for it how he would prepare his Sunday sermons. He would still be working on them on Saturday night. He would have his scripture commentaries and homiletic aids out on his desk, along with notes of his own and the newspapers of that week. He would stay up working until after midnight, sometimes until two or three in the morning. Sister Teresa would see him praying before retiring, and the next morning he would preach his homily. I think, then, that Archbishop Romero's final decision in all important matters was personal. I think that it often occurred to him personally what he ought to do, while at other times others made suggestions. Does not everyone have this experience? But the final decision was always his, and it was personal.

What really calls for analysis, it seems to me, is *why* Archbishop Romero made the decisions he made. And in order to be able to make this analysis, it seems to me appropriate to distinguish between, shall we say, the "major" and the "minor" pressures exerted on anyone. Minor pressures—the "categorical" ones, let us call them—are the thousand-and-one occurrences and contacts of daily life: conversations, discussions, possible annoyances, demands made by various persons. No one in the official church, from the pope to the simplest religion teacher, is exempt from these pressures. But the major pressures—the "transcendent" ones, let us say—are another matter. For Archbishop Romero, the transcendent pressures were the will of God and the suffering of the people. There is no doubt in my mind that, with the freedom he found bestowed upon him in his experience of God and his experience of the poor, Archbishop Romero was altogether willing to be "pressured" by these. If anything "manipulated" Archbishop Romero, it was the grace of God and the suffering of his people. It is these major, transcendent pressures that ultimately explain Archbishop Romero's life and work. The other pressures of life, the everyday, categorical ones, were part of his life as well, yes, but they were always secondary to the major pressures.

Why some persons would like to reduce Archbishop Romero to the product of manipulation is as obvious as it is tragic. Those who are unwilling to recognize his stature because he disturbs them or calls their lives into question look for a "reason why" Archbishop Romero was the way he was. Then they shall not be conscience-bound to imitate him. They look for excuses, but never logical or disinterested ones. Here again Archbishop Romero reminds me of Jesus. "He has lost his mind," some said of Jesus. "He is possessed by the devil," said others. "What do you expect? He's from Nazareth," jeered still others. They were dead set against following Jesus of Nazareth.

Archbishop Romero himself reflected on this kind of remark made about him, and we are fortunate to have his reflections on record. He expressed them publicly, in a homily on the fate of the prophets, July 8, 1979.

> This is the terrible thing about our society. It is a society that rejects the word of the gospel when that word does not suit its selfishness, when it does not suit its injustice. Suddenly a thousand questions arise. "Where does he get all these ideas? Who is manipulating him in this way? These can't be his own ideas!" And all of these foolish accusations, instead of becoming real questions ("Is he right or isn't he?"), remain purely rhetorical ones, and the victim is simply rejected.

It is sad to have to recall these things, and to have to observe that for some persons—even within the institutional church—Archbishop Romero was nothing but a product of manipulation in his lifetime, and nothing but an inflated myth in death. And it is sad not only because the appraisal is unjust, but because it is a sin against the light and therefore irremediable. If the good news comes and no response, no gratitude, no discipleship is forthcoming, but only tergiversation and rejection, then nothing will work a change. To me, Archbishop Romero is not an inflated myth or a product of manipulation. He had his limitations, as he himself noted in his retreat, but they were minor—very minor, from the spiritual viewpoint, and normal from the viewpoint of human psychology. But even with these limitations, Archbishop Romero was a Salvadoran, a believer, and an exceptional archbishop. So many persons, including important persons, who knew him, so many millions of persons who remember him today and who love him, cannot be mistaken on this point. As I have stated, if there was any manipulation, I believe and hope that Archbishop Romero manipulated us far more than we him.

All this talk of manipulation has pretty much died out — although Bishop Revelo of Santa Ana has brought it up again, and one Fredy Delgado, a priest of the diocese of San Vicente, has just published a pamphlet full of falsehoods in which this one is included. But something even sadder is now occurring in El Salvador. An attempt is under way to silence Archbishop Romero. Archbishop Romero is presumed to have been a great prophet, a martyr, even a saint — if the rumors are true that his cause is to be introduced — but of the *past*. Sad and unbelievable as it may seem, the Salvadoran Bishops Conference never makes any mention of him in its messages, never quotes his words of encouragement that they may inspire the Christians of today. Here Archbishop Romero is indeed dead and buried.

The reason given for this attempt to silence him is, once more, his alleged manipulation by the "left." While there is no longer so much insistence on his having been the product of manipulation by the left during his lifetime, it is now asserted that the left seeks to manipulate him for its own ends now that he is dead. And to prevent this, Archbishop Romero is subjected to the cruelest species of manipulation: silence. And the perpetrators of this deed even add: "Archbishop Romero is ours."

The question, "Who is Archbishop Romero?" can be answered only by way of honest analysis. Archbishop Romero was an archbishop, and so belongs to the hierarchical church. He was a Christian, and so belongs to all Christians. He was a Salvadoran, and so belongs to all Salvadorans. He was these three things in an outstanding way, and so can be taken as an example to follow by all three — and would that this should come to pass! — hierarchs, Christians, and Salvadorans. But to take Archbishop Romero as an example does not mean regarding him as private property — least of all in the sense of the talent in the parable that was buried to keep it from being lost. To take Archbishop Romero as an example means precisely to cease to keep him for ourselves and to put him to work, again like the talents of the gospel parable.

How many persons and groups here in El Salvador remember, love, and claim Archbishop Romero — base communities, groups of priests and nuns, union members, even the guerrillas of the FMLN (who celebrate March 24 in their camps)! Others are not pleased that things should be this way, but this is the way things are, and we must ask ourselves if it is objectively good or bad that they should be this way. In my judgment, as Archbishop Romero is both of God and of this world, an illustrious believer and an illustrious Salvadoran, all of those who have a genuine experience both of faith and of the reality of this world have a right to appeal to him, recall him, and celebrate him as theirs. Nor is this manipulation, as long as recalling either the sacred or secular dimension of Archbishop Romero does not mean rejecting the other. It is another matter who has the greatest right and greatest need to lay claim to him. These are those who invoke him as a Christian *and* as a Salvadoran: those Salvadorans who are poor and Christian, who find in him a light and hope that they find nowhere else, and who really love Archbishop Romero because he really loved them.

Manipulation of Archbishop Romero occurs when only one of these two dimensions of his is seized upon to the exclusion of the other. But the most despicable manipulation is that of his silencing, as if he no longer had anything to say, anything to offer his country and the church. Every now and then it is announced that there will be an investigation of his assassination. But this is to return only to his corpse, and not to his life. Of course, even more hypocritical than the triumphant proclamation that the government has solved this crime, when it makes no effort to solve the other sixty thousand murders of Salvadorans who held Archbishop Romero's principles; even worse than the attempted manipulation of publishing the results of these "investigations" during a political campaign (the party making the accusations seeking to place the blame on the other party) — the worst thing of all is that all of these self-servers are simply gathered around Archbishop Romero's dead body, waving their arms and shouting, while the living, enlightening, inspiring Archbishop Romero himself is gagged and silenced. Does Archbishop Romero have nothing to say today about the life and death of Salvadorans, about war and peace, about justice and reconciliation? Not one word of his is ever cited by the government, the Assembly, politicians, the armed forces, or the U.S. Embassy.

Does Archbishop Romero have nothing to say about faith, hope, and Christian commitment, about priestly and parish life, about prophecy and mercy? Archbishop Rivera, the only bishop who was loyal to him in life, does occasionally quote him. Archbishop Rivera's work of dialogue and negotiation, his cooperation in attempts to humanize our conflict and alleviate its consequences, the support he shows for the Archdiocesan Legal Advocacy Office, do reflect something of Archbishop Romero's inspiration. But the bishops conference ignores him. Diocesan pastoral plans ignore him (where they exist). This is the saddest of all of Archbishop Romero's funerals.

Still Archbishop Romero lives. He lives in the person of those who go to the cathedral to pray to him: he lives in the depths of their hearts. He lives in shelters, relocation camps, the remote regions of the country, the bowels of city slums. He lives in some religious, some professionals, and some intellectuals. At the University of Central America, posters everywhere bear his likeness. For me there is no doubt that Archbishop Romero lives in the poor, for whom life—and life in the basic, literal sense of sheer survival—continues to be the fundamental task. He lives in all of those who make a decision to serve the life of these peoples, and who rely on their memory of him for the courage to face the risks they must take. And he lives in all of those who, now groping, now exulting, seek God in the sincerity of their hearts. Archbishop Romero continues to be the light by which they contemplate the mystery of this God, such a dark mystery in the crucifixion of the poor, and such a luminous one in their hope of resurrection, to which they commit themselves with all their heart and soul.

X

These are some of my recollections of Archbishop Romero. I have mentioned only a few—the ones most important to me, the ones that have most enlightened and encouraged me. Other persons may have similar recollections. Still others will cherish different, perhaps more significant ones. Surely the basic recollection is the one stored up in the hearts of the poor—which, when all is said and done, I cannot penetrate. And were we to attempt to gather together, one by one, all of the recollections anyone has of Archbishop Romero, then surely, in the words of St. John at the end of his gospel, "the whole world could not contain the books that would have to be written" to record them.

I should like to add that I do not offer these recollections in the spirit of a panegyric. A papal nuncio once told me that I "overdid" my praise of Archbishop Romero when I wrote of him. I think that this is untrue even objectively. It is certainly untrue in my intent. But I cannot deny the profound impact that Archbishop Romero had on me.

I should also like to add that not all of my exceptional recollections from those exceptional years in El Salvador are of Archbishop Romero. I recall Rutilio Grande, as well, along with many other priests, sisters, *campesinos*, union members, and university students who were also put to death for justice' sake. Some of them died more painfully than did Archbishop Romero—tortured to death. Recalling Archbishop Romero, then, does not mean isolating him from the other martyrs of our country, or exalting him in such a way as to leave the others in the shade. No, to recall Archbishop Romero is precisely to recall so many others as well—so many prophets and martyrs, so many *campesinos* and Delegates of the Word, all of them preachers, by their deeds, of the living word of God. And above all, to recall Archbishop Romero means recalling thousands of innocent, defenseless, and nameless martyrs: it means recalling an entire crucified people, whose names will never be publicly known, but who now are one with Archbishop Romero forever. He who in life was the voice of the voiceless, in death is the name of the nameless. God grant that one day we may see the canonization of "Archbishop Romero and the Salvadoran Martyrs," or "Archbishop Romero and the Latin American Martyrs."

In conclusion, then, I should like to insist that my recollections of Archbishop Romero surely have meaning only within the one great recollection of the whole Archbishop Romero. The recollections that I have offered are not intended as material for a biography of the life of this illustrious personage, this excellent human being. They are not like the pieces of a puzzle that only make a picture when you put enough of them together.

On the contrary, to me the picture has always been perfectly clear, and alone gives meaning to the pieces. I may have gathered up the several pieces of the picture more or less adequately (although, in all honesty, I have made no attempt to do so). Or others may now come by with entirely different pieces, and thereby clarify (or dispute) the meaning of the pieces I have presented. I willingly accept either eventuality.

Might I be permitted to attempt to sum up in a single word the whole of Archbishop Romero? Could there ever be a one-word answer to the question, "Who was Archbishop Romero?" In the New Testament, after Jesus' death and resurrection, the various evangelists answered the question, "Who was Jesus?" in different ways. Some of them called him Messiah, others Son of God, others Word of God. And of course they were all correct. For my part, I have called Archbishop Romero a shepherd, a prophet, a martyr, a great believer, and a great Salvadoran. But if I had to sum up in a single word and concept the truth expressed by all of these titles together, I should have to say: Archbishop Romero was a gospel. Archbishop Romero was a piece of good news from God to the poor of this world, and then, from this starting point in the poor, to all men and women. To put it another way—an even more radical way, theologically speaking—I should like to close this introductory chapter with the words Father Ignacio Ellacuría used to describe Archbishop Romero in his homily at the Mass we concelebrated at Central American University only a few days after his martyrdom. They are engraved on my heart. "With Archbishop Romero, God has visited El Salvador."

PART 1

Theological Analysis of Archbishop Romero's Person and Work

CHAPTER 2

Archbishop Romero: Believer, Archbishop, Salvadoran*

His Gospel Faith

Archbishop Romero became a quite exceptional figure in Latin America, both within the church and within society at large. To understand this, I want to begin by examining something deeper, something of which the social and ecclesial dimensions of his life were the expression, the vehicle. I want to plumb what is the ultimate mystery of every human being, that which is hidden in the depths of the heart, that source from which emanate both our daily lives and the actions we take at crucial moments. I want, in other words, to plumb that most simple yet most sublime thing we call faith.

Perhaps it appears to be saying little, or saying something very obvious, if I begin by describing Romero as a man who believed in God. So little has the word *God* come to mean that it is easily taken for granted that everyone believes in God. On the other hand God can be so readily ignored that no longer does it seem to render particular honor to Romero's memory,

---

*Written immediately following Archbishop Romero's death and first published as "Monseñor Romero: Mártir de la liberación: Análisis teológico de su figura y obra," *Estudios Centroamericanos,* March 1980, pp. 253–76. The translation, by Michael J. Walsh, is from *Voice of the Voiceless* (Maryknoll, N.Y.: Orbis Books, 1985).

or to provide an adequate theological basis upon which to begin, simply to say that he believed in God.

Yet in its Christian fullness, *God* is a far from empty term. It is far from a remote, passive abstraction. Quite the opposite. God is the prime source of all life, justice, love, and truth, and the ultimate horizon to which all these reach out. It is God who lays upon us the absolute demand that we live our lives in a way truly worthy of human beings, that we strive always to make ourselves more human by continually ridding ourselves of that which makes us less human.

The first thing I want to say of Archbishop Romero, therefore, is that he had a profound faith in God. We know of the devotion, felt not feigned, with which he spoke of God in his homilies. We know of his spirit of meditation and his simple, down-to-earth prayers. For him, to speak with God was something as straightforward and routine as life itself.

I also want to say of Archbishop Romero that he believed in God as did Jesus. That is why I want to examine his following of Jesus precisely from the standpoint of his faith. Like Jesus, to be in communion with God, to speak with God and to speak about God, meant above all making God's will concrete and effective. The measure of Romero's faith can be gauged by the way he utterly and completely defended God's cause. Like Jesus he sought and found God's will as much in the minutiae of everyday life as in life's most profound and significant moments. He never made of God's will something trivial or routine, as all of us Christians—bishops and priests included—do only too often. We—and the church itself—lay down rules and regulations today, just as was done in the time of Jesus. We try to cut God down to size, to manipulate, even to downgrade God. Romero placed no limits to God's will. On the contrary, he sought the will of God where it is in truth to be found: where the lives of men and women hang in the balance, where sin turns human beings into slaves, and where there hence arises a cry for justice, and the hope for society and for the oppressed that is growing in the world. It is that that I shall explain in what follows.

The God of the Kingdom

Archbishop Romero's faith in God made him a defender of life, and especially a defender of the lives of the poor. The anguish of the poor touches the very heart of God. That is why Romero saw in life, and in life at its most basic, the manifestation of God, as did the prophet Isaiah before him. The world of food and work, of health and housing, the world of education — this is God's world. The world God wants is one in which "they will build houses and inhabit them, plant vineyards and eat their fruit" (Isa. 65:21). Poverty and desolation are a denial of God's will, a perverted creation in which God's glory is mocked and scorned. Belief in the fullness of the life to come is no palliative or opiate: faith in God begins with the defense of life here and now. The living person is God's glory. To be absolutely accurate, the living, poor man or woman is God's glory (Louvain address, February 2, 1980).[1]

Because of his faith in God, Archbishop Romero denounced El Salvador's sin with a fierceness that can be likened only to that of the prophets of old, or to that of Bartolomé de Las Casas, or to that of Jesus himself. Hardship, he declared, is not the natural destiny of the people of El Salvador. It is, at root, the outcome of unjust structures. With unequalled ferocity he lashed out at the repression mounted against the people, the massacres, the genocide.

Romero never ceased in his attack, he never tempered it, he never found prudent reasons for silence. Unlike others, he never put the church's own security before the necessity of attacking repression. He had heard God saying, "You may multiply your prayers, I shall not listen. Your hands are covered with blood" (Isa. 1:15).

Sin for him was an offense against God *because* it is an offense against the people. Sin is indeed something that causes death — that is why it is called mortal. One cannot *see* an offense against God: it becomes visible when one sees blood-stained corpses, when one hears the wailing of the mothers of those who have disappeared, and of the tortured. Because his faith was in the God of life, such sin was utterly counter to his faith. His faith bore him up in his denunciation of sin. It added to the harshness with which he exposed it. It enabled him to ignore the risks, both personal and institutional, that he had to run.

Through his faith in God, Archbishop Romero worked and struggled toward a just solution to his country's problems. He believed in the God of the exodus who today as yesterday looks upon a captive and exploited people, hears their cries, then comes to free them, and to promise them a new land.

But Romero also believed that this liberating will of God had to be made effective. He was not content, therefore, simply to speak in favor of life and to denounce all that opposed it. Instead he placed himself clearly on the side of justice — that is to say, on the side of the struggle to win a decent way of life for the poor. He did not rely on purely political considerations, but on his faith in God. That is why he did not stop where others stopped: at conflict and the organization of the poor.

He was a man of peace. He was always in favor of peaceful solutions. But his faith brought him to accept the mystery of conflict to which sin gives rise. He accepted that sin can be overcome only by a struggle against it. Like Mary he accepted calmly that God "has pulled down princes from their thrones and exalted the lowly" (Luke 1:52). Some Pharisaically see a source of scandal in the fact of conflict. For Romero his acceptance of it was a demand made upon him by his faith in God.

And because he believed in a God who wills justice, Romero also embraced that other fact of life from which others hold themselves back — the fact that the poor have to liberate themselves, that they have to take charge of their own destiny, and not simply be passive recipients of benefits that descend from "above." He came to understand that in El Salvador that which is above is made up of the gods of unbridled capitalism and "national security" and that the God of liberation has to be met "below." It was because of that belief that Romero backed all just movements of the people that carried them toward freedom.

Romero believed in the God of the Kingdom today in El Salvador just as Jesus had proclaimed it in his own day: a just society for all men and women, and especially for the poor. He believed that the battle for this new society had to be joined, and he believed that that society ought to be one *of* new men and women, *of* men and women of the Kingdom. He therefore never lost sight of the moral and spiritual dimensions of the people. He encouraged the view that even in conflict and battle there could be true human values — those of solidarity, generosity, clarity of vision; values, in a word, that Jesus proclaimed in the Sermon on the Mount. And even in just struggle he was critical, as a pastor, of all that might dehumanize human nature.

He was not guided in any way by political calculations, much less by thought of the popularity—or notoriety—to which his preaching about the values of the Kingdom gave rise. He was guided by an unshakable faith in a God who wills a new kind of society and a new kind of human person. Even though the attainment of such a society may have been a lost cause, he time and again urged purity of heart, magnanimity, dialogue, and an openness to one's own conversion. He also spoke for things that few today in El Salvador can mention without cynicism: forgiveness and overcoming the instinct for vengeance.

No one who knew Archbishop Romero would see in his exhortations any naiveté or the routine repetition of Christian verities. They would see rather a deep faith in God, a faith that pointed toward the utopia of the Kingdom of God and of the people of the Kingdom. He was well aware of the problems standing in the way of the achievement of both these utopias, but he never lost heart. He tirelessly proclaimed and promoted them because he believed in God's utopia and because he believed that such a utopia—even though it might never be fully realized—was the best way of bringing about humankind's greater humanity.

The God of Truth

Because of his faith in God, Archbishop Romero associated his struggle for justice with the proclamation of the truth. No one spoke out as much and as clearly about the dire situation in El Salvador. Shortly before his martyrdom he was able to say, as in his own day Jesus too had said, that in more than two years of preaching no one could ever accuse him of lying.

This love for, and ceaseless preaching of, the truth had a profoundly humanizing effect throughout the country. In the first place, it was not that the archbishop merely told the truth: he told the whole truth. In crisis situations it sometimes—if infrequently—happens that the truth is told. It is very rare indeed for the whole truth to be told, because this presupposes not only telling the truth but experiencing the demands that it makes on one. It presupposes that alongside the truth there shall go the struggle for liberation. It also makes the truth a weapon in that struggle. It takes for granted that in the truth there is something that cannot be manipulated, that the effectiveness of the truth lies in its very telling. It is in this sense that Romero was an impassioned teller of the truth.

Secondly, simply by speaking the truth Romero gave its value back to the silenced, manipulated, distorted word. He made the word what it ought to be: the expression of reality. His Sunday sermons were listened to because in them the real situation of the country found expression. In his preaching the daily hopes and griefs that the media usually either ignored or distorted found expression. No Salvadoran can any longer ignore the fact that the word, dialogue, speech have to be at the service of objective reality, not of partisan interests.

That love for the truth, that putting into words of the real state of affairs, was rooted in Romero's faith in God. The phrase used by Christians at the end of the scripture readings, "This is the word of the Lord," was not a mere saying for him. It was an urgent commitment to go on preaching the word and using it to bring before hearers the real situation of the country. "The word of God is not in chains," said St. Paul. For Romero it would have been a fearsome crime to have tied down, or to have ignored, that word both as it is to be found in Scripture and as it is to be found in the events of history. So he spoke, and spoke the truth. He believed that God is also the God of truth. He saw in the truths made manifest in history an indication of God's demands upon us, and a manifestation of God in history.

The God of Change

Because of his faith in God, Romero was not alarmed by changes that took place. Rather he made of change a vehicle for his faith. At a strictly personal level he knew how to grow, to change, even how to undergo conversion. The beginning of his ministry in the archdiocese coincided with the beginning of the persecution of the church and intensified repression of the people. He was changed by this new situation, he was converted. He was fifty-nine years old. Most person's psychological attitudes and mental patterns have already been formed by that age. He was, moreover, at the head of the church's institutional authority, an authority that, like all others, tends toward establishment and immobility. Yet even from that position and at that age he demonstrated the true humility of those who believe in God. He became someone new. He was driven on by a new and different sense of what it meant to be a Christian. He understood his ministry as a bishop in a wholly new way.

Taking on his new office he began new forms of pastoral activity. He even adopted a new theology, much to the surprise and alarm of those who preferred the old, the known, that with which they felt secure. He was concerned with the new problems that the history of the church and of his country put before him. He did not choose in advance which problems to respond to, feeling safest with traditional ones. Quite the opposite: he faced up to new situations as they arose. To the very end he was concerned with what he called his apostolate of companionship to politically committed Christians, with the changing situation in El Salvador, and with the future—as shown by his keen interest in events in Nicaragua. He was as much surprised as anyone else by the changes that history brought. He was displeased by his feeling of impotence, of being unable to think of an answer immediately. But he was never brought to a dead stop. He was encouraged to go on seeking the will of God in all the twists and turns of history.

His openness to change, his facing up to the challenge of the new, was simply the expression of his faith in a God whose mystery, as John says, is greater than our hearts, greater than any particular situation. Romero readily accepted that God was also present in the old, certainly in God's revelation in Scripture and in the traditions of the church. That is why he was so scrupulously faithful to Vatican II, to Medellín, and to Puebla. But the same conviction made him faithful to the Spirit of God, a Spirit not to be encapsulated in the traditions of the church; one that blows when and where it wills. The when and the where have always to be sought out anew. There are no ready-made "traveler's guidebooks."

Because of his faith in the God of change, Archbishop Romero often had to journey alone, misunderstood by many of those around him, even by other bishops. He knew only that, like Abraham, he had to travel a road with trust in the Spirit of God. He knew that God is greater than all the roads already traveled, and that God cannot be localized definitively. Romero heard God's word, "Leave your country, your family and your father's house, for the land I will show you" (Gen. 12:1). To believe in God meant for Romero to take that saying seriously, not reducing it to something manageable but letting God be ever a God of change, following wheresoever the Spirit of God might lead.

The God of the Poor

Because of that faith, Archbishop Romero encountered in the midst of the poor the pathway to belief in God. I am here speaking not so much of the good he did for the poor—I will examine that more closely later—but rather the good the poor did for him, as far as his faith was concerned.

In the first place he found in the poor that which is scandalous in the mystery of God understood in a Christian sense: in those whom history crucifies is made present the crucified God. The kenotic dimension of God—God's self-emptying, in other words—goes on being foolishness, a scandal. It is the dividing line between authentic Christianity and other theistic beliefs. It is made manifest in the poor, in the oppressed and the repressed of God's people. In their faces Romero saw the disfigured countenance of God.

And he encountered God from the perspective of the poor. The problem of the locus where God might be found presented itself to him as the problem of finding a perspective from which, afterward, God might always be found no matter what the situation. In hermeneutical theology that question is a matter of complex debate. Romero resolved it very simply. His deep conviction can best be expressed in a sentence from the Puebla documents: "Therefore, because they are poor, God comes to their defense and loves them" (1142). There is stated here a particular relationship between God and the poor, a *preferential* relationship within the overall relationship between God and creation. The beneficiaries of this partiality are those who, in their turn, can point out the locus of the correct relationship with God.

This does not mean that Romero idealized the poor. It means that he had found the locus where something fundamental about God may be learned. He had discovered the perspective from which one can determine in a particular place and time the criteria for building up the Kingdom—the place of truth and the direction of change. Precisely from this particular perspective one can overcome the superficial generalization that God can be found everywhere and in whatever manner. Through his partiality for the poor, Romero could be impartial—and find God everywhere.

It is the Christian paradox that the mystery of the great God is first shown in what is tiny, what is least. And it is from that least place that God is shown ever greater. That is why one can say that the poor preached the gospel to Archbishop Romero. He was preached to by way of those positive values that are very often to be found among the poor. They so situated him that he could correctly hear the good news of God.

Father of Jesus

In describing the faith that Romero had, I have been describing the Father of Jesus. The God of the Kingdom, the God of truth, the God of change, the God of the poor—these are phrases that describe Jesus' God. I should like to bring this short analysis to a close by considering two features of Jesus' attitude to his Father that Romero shared.

Faith is a gift. But faith was not given to Romero once and for all. Like Jesus he was open to temptation. He had to endure loneliness, ignorance, attack, and persecution. He had to preserve his faith. Like Jesus he had to go on practicing it—through ecclesial and historical tasks that for him were the tasks of the episcopal ministry and a leadership that reached into civil society, as we shall see in greater detail further on.

It is not only that Romero had faith in God, he was also a faithful witness to the end. He became for many Christians what is said of Jesus in the Letter to the Hebrews—though of Jesus in all plenitude: "[he] leads us in our faith and brings it to perfection" (12:2).

He believed in Jesus' God, and he believed the way Jesus did. Here is the gospel basis for his life and work, the basis of his impressive human qualities. I began this analysis of his life and work with his gospel faith because that is the way that one can most readily come to understand his impact both as archbishop and as a leader in society. In effect it is impossible easily to distinguish between these two dimensions, between his personal faith and his ministry, because they were dialectically linked. His faith was the foundation for his actions, but in turn his actions concretized his faith. There is no doubt that without the gift of faith, and without the quality of his faith, it is impossible fundamentally to comprehend the quality of his public ministry.

His Episcopal Ministry

Romero was not only a believer, a follower of Jesus. He was in addition an archbishop. It seems to me to be very important indeed to insist that it was through his episcopal ministry that his faith took concrete shape, and not despite that ministry, or in isolation from it.

There is no doubt that episcopacy is one of the crucial aspects of the church as an institution. Equally there is no doubt that the institutional church is going through a serious crisis precisely because of its incapacity to act as an adequate vehicle for a vibrant faith.

Romero knew how to bring faith and episcopacy—personal charism and the institution—together. It was a remarkable gift, and an uncommon one, though he shared it with a number of Latin American bishops of today. I want, in describing Romero as a bishop, to do justice to his work. But indirectly this presentation could also be an aid to the theology of the episcopate, something particularly necessary nowadays.

Confirming the Faith of His Brothers and Sisters

This duty, conferred by Jesus on St. Peter, Archbishop Romero carried out to perfection, and with surprising repercussions.

The faith of the archdiocese has undoubtedly grown and deepened. Rural and urban working-class families have made more profound their traditional, popular religion. The middle class, whose faith had been little more than conventional, or whose superficial liberalism had driven them out of the church, has again begun to show its faith in the gospel. At the level of the archdiocesan collective consciousness, the faith has been reevaluated.

This owes a good deal to Archbishop Romero. He learned the lesson well that, as bishop, it was his duty to confirm the faith of his brothers and sisters. And he learned it in a very down-to-earth way. He came to realize that this basic ministry that he had to exercise as bishop is neither identical with, nor can it be adequately fulfilled through, his teaching office. That is to say, it cannot be fulfilled simply by preserving, explaining, and interpreting the formulas of faith. He did not neglect the teaching office, as we shall see later. But he understood that faith is prior to the magisterium, that the life of faith takes precedence over the *formulations* of faith. In the ministry of confirming others in the faith he saw something that was both deeper than, and prior to, the ministry of teaching. He tried to strengthen the faith of his brothers and sisters in that which is central to, which sums up, the faith: the following of Jesus.

It was the bishop's task, as he understood it, to make the Christian faith "credible" at its deepest level. But he also understood that he should not do this, in the first instance, simply by using the full weight of his authority to proclaim the faith, or to demand it of others. He had to make the faith actual in himself. He had to progress in faith, remain loyal to it, live it out in concrete situations, accept the risks that go along with trying to live it out.

The essential mark of the office of bishop is to be a witness to the faith, truly and deeply. A bishop ought to be such that the faithful believe what he believes, and to believe in such a way that they feel themselves nourished and strengthened in their faith. Every Christian is called upon to be a witness of the faith. But given the prominence of his office, and the opportunities that it provides, it is the special role of the bishop, and his grave responsibility, explicitly to be such a witness.

Defender of the Poor and Oppressed

It was not that he simply imitated Jesus, as do so many other Christians. No, he made the defense of the poor and oppressed a specific and basic function of his episcopal ministry. His pastoral activity clearly put him on their side. He denounced the destitution from which they suffered, and its causes. He identified himself with them. He defended their interests. At the administrative level he had the human and material resources of the archdiocese redistributed to their benefit.

In analyzing his episcopacy it is essential to realize that he made of the defense of the poor his principal ministry. He restored what had been one of the most important aspects of the episcopacy when it was introduced at the time of the colonization, but which was afterward lost. At the time of the colonization the bishop was *ex officio* the "protector of the Indians." On the assumption—very real, as it turned out—that the Indians were going to be marginalized, exploited, and decimated, the bishop had the task of protecting them, defending them from exploitation by either the military or the colonists.

This deeply Christian and ecclesial insight into the role of a bishop, which goes back four centuries, was revived in our day by Romero. The poor, the oppressed, anyone in need knew this, and turned to him for help. They came to the archbishop when they wanted injustices denounced, their rights asserted, missing persons found. They came to him to mediate when lands had been seized or when the security forces had surrounded churches. It was not that they came to him simply as a friend, seeking consolation. They came to him as a protector who was in duty bound to put the full weight of his episcopal authority at the service of the poor and oppressed.

If the poor came to him spontaneously, it was because he had himself projected that image of what it meant to be a bishop. In doing so he achieved something of the greatest importance— though it may seem, when put down on paper, a little ambiguous. What he succeeded in doing was "institutionalizing" the preferential option for the poor. To "institutionalize," in this instance, does not mean to bureaucratize or trivialize. On the contrary, it means that not only should Christians as individuals make this option for the poor, but so should the church as such, placing at the disposal of the poor the resources that the church, as an institution, has at its own disposal.

Precisely because he was the archbishop and therefore the foremost representative of the institutional church, it became possible to speak of the church of the poor. Because of him the people could judge the various ecclesiastical institutions by that criterion: the defense of the poor and the oppressed.

Evangelist to the Whole Country

Romero fulfilled Jesus' command to his apostles to make a disciple of everyone. He was conscious of the fact that, as archbishop, it was his duty to respond to the "everyone" of the gospel. He had to evangelize the whole population of El Salvador as it then was.

Because both the archdiocese and the nation were small, and their problems similar, the task of evangelizing the whole population was made easier. The archbishop's prestige, and his use of the media, meant that he could reach out into every corner of the land. His evangelization of the whole of El Salvador was based on three principles.

1. It meant, first, to preach the gospel to all, to try to proclaim the good news to everyone, no matter what their personal and social situation. Romero was well aware that even by pastoral, let alone social and economic, criteria, the population was divided into distinct groups. So he undertook his apostolate in different ways, not only as to the means he used, but even in the purpose and direction of his evangelization. In his apostolate among the masses he took into account the need to purify and reinforce popular religion. His apostolate to politically committed Christians took the form of encouragement. Vis-à-vis those Christians in positions of economic or political power, however, his apostolate was to work for their conversion.

2. To preach the gospel to all also meant to evangelize the "structural reality," the country as a whole seen not just as the sum of all those who make it up but in terms of the structures that condition the lives of everyone living there. Romero preached the gospel in this sense, denouncing unjust structures,

calling attention to the changes—whether social, economic, or political—that were needed, and promoting the particular projects that seemed most likely to bring about the required changes. He saw clearly that, at the present time, the church has to associate "preaching the gospel to everyone" with "evangelizing the whole of the country in all its social, economic, and political aspects."

3. To evangelize the whole population also meant to understand adequately the ecclesiastical function of small groups within the church, while avoiding the temptation of reducing the church to such groups. Clearly, small groups will always spring up, whether in the traditional forms of religious congregations, or in the form of lay movements, or in the more modern form of basic Christian communities. They should be thought of here in relation to the purpose of preaching the gospel. At bottom, there are two theoretical models of basic Christian communities.

According to one model, the church should promote these groups, take refuge in them, find in them the last stronghold of the faith where the human and Christian needs of a very small number of individuals can be satisfied. This model implies reductionism and, at root, the collapse of the church. It regards these groups as a way of saving all that can be saved of the church.

According to the second model, Christian groups arise out of mass evangelization. Basic communities spring up within the context of local problems and in light of the need to establish the Kingdom of God. They arise in response to a need, and as a means of fulfilling it. Hence this model is not so much a "reduction" as a "concentration." The church is concentrated in these groups. The purpose is not so much to attend better to the needs of a few, but to be a better leaven to all.

The fundamental difference between the two models is that, according to the first, the church would go on being turned in on itself, and in the second it would be at the service of the Kingdom. In fact, of course, neither model exists in its pure form. I want simply to draw attention to the fact that precisely because Archbishop Romero wanted to evangelize the whole population, he encouraged the second, rather than the first, of the two models of basic communities—a term, incidentally, that can also be used of lay movements or religious congregations. In his heart of hearts, however, he believed that the evangelization of the few, and a form of Christian life that could serve only the needs of a few, profoundly contradicted the word of God addressed to all, and that such a contradiction put in doubt the efficacy of that word.

He understood evangelization to be something that ought to be expressed through every aspect of the church's life, both in its this-worldly and in its transcendental aspects, in personal and in social terms, in its liturgical and educational life, and so on. To the totality there to be evangelized, the church ought to address itself with the totality of its being. Archbishop Romero did not himself develop a particular theory of evangelization. He was inspired by Paul VI's apostolic exhortation *Evangelii Nuntiandi*. He put it into practice and, at several points, he added to it. He lived it out in his own apostolate and he impressed upon his pastoral agents that they too should implement it.

He attached great importance to the proclamation of the word. Both through his own Christian conviction and through his personal charism as a preacher, he made the word his most important instrument as an evangelist. He proclaimed the word as the word of God, and in his homilies dwelt long upon explaining it. But it is important to add that he believed the word of God was still manifesting itself today, in "the signs of the times." Moreover he believed that the very proclamation of the word had its own particular efficacy. It is not only a telling of truths, it is truth itself. And that is why it is effective: it makes present that which it proclaims.

He gave high priority to making the word come true, to turning the good news into a good reality. In the third part of this essay I shall show how he turned this proclamation of the word into a force for social transformation. What I want to stress here is that he did not reduce making the word come true simply to the ethical level, so that he fulfilled his evangelizing mission merely by proclaiming the word. He realized that making the word actual is an essential part of evangelization. There was in his preaching a dialectic between the proclamation and the realization of good news, in such a way that each helped explain the other.

He also regarded as supremely important the manner of preaching: the testimony of one's own life — in other words, the holiness of the preacher. Just as he believed in the Kingdom of God and the people of the Kingdom, so too he believed that the efficacy of preaching went hand in hand with the credibility of the preacher. His most valuable contribution here was his concretization of the concept of holiness. Preachers certainly ought to possess the Christian virtues, the marks of a follower of Jesus. But as preachers they ought to give a yet more fundamental witness: they must not abandon their people, they must travel along with them and, like good shepherds, be ready to lay down their life for them.

These three aspects of evangelization are to be found in *Evangelii Nuntiandi*. Archbishop Romero emphasized a fourth element: prophetic denunciation. He was renowned in this regard both for his unequalled courage and for his solid incorruptibility. It is important to stress that he even saw denunciation as good news, a sort of gospel *sub specie contrarii.* He proclaimed the good news by negating what was evil. Sin he always denounced with great harshness, but he always managed to keep the accent on good news when speaking to oppressors. They, too, were his brothers and sisters. The good news was intended for them too; it beckoned them to conversion.

For their part the powerful, the ruling elite, the capitalists, reacted violently against him. As they had once said of Jesus that he was mad, that he was a new Beelzebub, that he was a political agitator trying to stir up the masses, so they now spoke of Romero. Money was poured out to belittle and calumniate him. Rarely can there have been so irrational and violent a campaign against a prophet. But Romero saw it all as part of the price a true prophet has to pay. He took it as evidence that what he stood for was the truth. But equally he saw in those who mounted the campaign persons to whom the gospel was also addressed. Like Jesus, he warned them against their unjust wealth. As he so vividly put it: "Pull the rings off your fingers before they cut off your hands." Like Jesus, he strove always to hold out to them the promise of true happiness, such as was given to Zacchaeus after his conversion: "Today the blessing has come upon this house."

The overarching of his work of evangelization was the cathedral, "his" cathedral. He had no property of his own, as his will demonstrated, but the cathedral was especially dear to him. He saw in it a symbol of the church and of the nation, in all their nobility and in all their tragedy. He made the cathedral his work place par excellence, the place where the people met, the place that linked hundreds of priests and nuns, the place from which his message went out to the nation, and to the nations of the world. But the cathedral has also been the place where persons have been massacred, the place where they have sought sanctuary. It has been a hospital for the wounded, a mortuary for the dead of the church and of the people. Several times the cathedral has been seized by popular organizations, several times closed and opened. It has been a place for the liturgy — and for hunger strikes.

This cathedral, this symbol of sorrow and of hope, a meeting place for the church and for the people, Romero made his own. Before the bodies of the dead he bolstered the hopes of the people. He wanted the cathedral to be what it ought above all to be: the chair from which was proclaimed the good news, the gospel. By nature he was rather shy. But in the cathedral he was transfigured. In it he became aware that the gospel was directed to all Salvadorans, to the whole of the country. He made the cathedral the center both of the church and of the nation. It will never be possible to write the history of the church or of the nation without telling the story of Archbishop Romero's cathedral.

Romero and the Teaching Office of the Bishop

It is obvious that, at the present time, this particular aspect of the episcopal ministry has its problems. Believers are not as ready as they once were to accept the magisterium. But it is also obvious, and especially in Latin America, that many episcopal documents have been issued that are truly inspirational, and are giving a new meaning to the teaching office. As a teacher of the truth, Romero was one of the bishops who helped bring this about. He was well aware of the grave responsibility involved in teaching. He was aware both of the difficulty of, and the need for, this role, and of the need, even for a bishop, of "learning to teach."

He knew how to link the church's general teaching—whether at the Latin American level (Medellín and Puebla) or at the worldwide level (Vatican II and papal encyclicals)—to the situation in El Salvador. He demonstrated this ability both in his four pastoral letters, which were on the whole doctrinal, as well as in his Sunday sermons, which were more catechetical in style. It was not an a priori fidelity to the church's documents that brought this about; he achieved it because he looked for, and found, the truths expressed in them. He understood that in what others have taught in the past there is truth to be found—though obviously to different degrees—and that there is still a demand for the truth today. He did not harmonize the church's teaching with conditions in El Salvador simply by applying universally applicable documents to concrete situations. He looked instead for the light that a truth already expressed might shed upon the truth that is to be sought in a new context. He found illumination in already written documents because he looked for it from within a particular situation.

Romero experienced the demands made upon him by the truth. In other words, it was not he who chose the problems with which he had to deal: he tackled those that history put before him, however novel and difficult they might be. He taught what it made sense to teach, what the situation demanded, and even about matters on which there was no ready-made and "safe" doctrine. Objective truth was not the only criterion for his magisterium: relevance was also a criterion. And because his pastoral letters do not simply contain general truths but are relevant as well, they have been widely distributed, and even translated into other languages.

In fulfilling his office of teacher, Romero was pastorally oriented. This was reflected in the manner of his teaching—in his firmness and in his humility. He was firm when he was clear on an issue; he was humble when the solution to a new problem was, by its very nature, provisional: more a search for, than a possession of, the truth. It was for that reason that his pastoral letter on popular organizations was put forward as the first stage in a dialogue, which, in the nature of the case, had to be continued.

He taught with episcopal authority, but not with episcopal exclusivity. He did not shirk ultimate responsibility, but he was in continual consultation with experts in the social sciences, with theologians, with analysts of the national situation and its wider setting. Above all, he took account of the people. He tried to answer the real questions that grassroots Christians asked, and took their opinions into consideration when he replied. Instance the questionnaire he circulated in the basic communities in the archdiocese before setting off for Puebla.

Finally, he taught to the extent that he went on learning. He gave the impression of putting forward a truth that was, of its very nature, always open to further refinement, and even to change, so that he always held himself open to learn. The continual refinement of his teaching was not only the consequence of development in the realm of theory—though that certainly played its part—but also because he kept in touch with the situation in the church and in society. He learned from the context in which he found himself. He learned as a Christian because he truly believed in a God who goes on being revealed in history. That is why he taught as he learned. It is no paradox to say that Archbishop Romero taught to the extent that he was taught by the world about him. He united in himself the heavy responsibility of teaching with the equally heavy responsibility of learning, and in doing so he exemplified something that is of the greatest importance for the office of bishop.

Head of the Body of the Archdiocese

The archdiocese of San Salvador could not be understood without him—but then neither could he be understood outside the context of the archdiocese. At the theoretical level, the ecclesial reality of the archdiocese can be thought of as a body, with the archbishop as the head. Under Archbishop Romero that theory became a reality.

As he himself confessed, right at the beginning of his archiepiscopal ministry, he was given the very best that the archdiocese could offer. The martyrdom of Father Grande, the support of the majority of the clergy, and, above all, contact with the sufferings of the people—all these changed him. Over three long years of persecution the courage of Salvadoran Christians, their sufferings and their faith, were molding the archbishop himself. It is in this sense one can say of Romero that he was indeed a symbol, a sign of the best that Christianity has to offer. True though it be that he brought with him to the office those human and Christian qualities already described, in a very real sense the Christian community formed the archbishop.

There was a real link, and not simply a chain of command, between the archbishop and the archdiocese. This link explains both the unity of the church and the creation of a team of evangelists. Romero brought about a rare unity within the archdiocese. Never before had there been such a common sense of purpose among priests, religious, and pastoral workers. But this unity was not all-encompassing.

There was a right-wing minority among pastoral workers in opposition to the archbishop. There were also those who wanted to go further than Romero in involving the church in social and political life. Toward both groups he was understanding but firm. Those on the right almost entirely abandoned him; with those on the left he kept up a dialogue right to the end, listening to them and learning from them.

The unity worked. Tensions were inevitable, but the archbishop managed to make them fruitful tensions, ones that moved forward. The archdiocese was united around its mission—that of evangelization. It was not turned in upon itself and concerned with purely ecclesiastical issues. The unity was, moreover, cemented by suffering and persecution. Yet this mission was also a source of disunity, not only within the archdiocese but even among the country's bishops, some of the clergy, and Christians who belonged to the ruling classes. To give Romero his due, it was not he who dissociated himself from them, but they who cut themselves off from him. It was not his personality that brought it about—he was always kindness and humility itself. Rather it was the mission of the church of which he was the leader. What most deeply saddened him was the division in the hierarchy. Because of the scandal it gave to the faithful it seriously worried him. It impoverished the church's mission in the country and gave support to those who criticized the church. But he put fidelity to his apostolate to the poor, as he saw it, before the anguish of disunion.

This very real unity within the church found expression in Romero's enormous ability for gathering the church together. This was certainly demonstrated when he said Mass, but it was also evident in other church activities. That unity was a real source of strength to the pastoral team made up of priests, nuns, catechists, minsters of the word, and others. Salvadorans understood that the whole of the archdiocese, and Romero himself, was behind all the church's activities.

It is in this sense — a sense that is historical and effective, not simply legal or abstract — that we can say Romero was the head of the archdiocese. He was the expression of all that was best and most Christian among the people. They saw him as their true representative. In this profound sense Romero let himself be made a bishop by his people, and they were grateful to him that he made them truly the body of the church.

Romero and the Institutional Power of the Church

It is clear that, at least in Latin America, the church is still a great social force. But this force can be used in many different ways. At one extreme it would be possible to use politico-ecclesiastical means to influence society, or to impose rules and regulations upon society from above. The other extreme would be to reduce the church to a community that abandons the world to its fate, or merely tries to change the world by the subjective testimony of holiness.

Archbishop Romero exercised an institutional power, but one different from both those extremes. He never wished to become one of the nation's important leaders, but he found himself a mediator, sometimes an arbiter, in a great variety of conflicts within society. Groups of very different tendencies turned to him for help. It is important to examine what Romero thought about this power and, given that he did not reject it, to see how he used it. It is also important to see how he reconciled institutional power with power put to the service of the poor, the majority of the population.

Romero certainly did not understand the church's institutional power in the first sense outlined above. The church's institutional power ought not to be thought of as analogous to state power in such a way that it might be regarded as natural that the church enter into dialogue with the state, the people simply being on the receiving end of the power exercised from above by both entities. In terms of this model, the ideal for Christianity would be for the church as institution to be on good terms with the state, avoiding all clashes with it, or resolving all such clashes to the people's cost.

Romero negated this model by the way he lived. The masses were not only not the beneficiaries of state handouts; they were the beneficiaries of no handouts at all. It was neither a power *of* the people, nor a power *for* the people that was exercised over them. The church, therefore, could not make peace with the system. And it had itself been directly persecuted by the state.

Romero broke with the model of church power as analogous to state power in a great number of ways. For example, he took part in no ceremony, political or ecclesiastical, that would have presented the two powers as being on the same footing and coexisting in supposed harmony. That is why, as he put it so graphically, the church had no problems with the state—only the people had problems. He wanted to make it clear that one should not think of the institutional authority of the church as power "from above," as similar to state power, and as the natural dialogue partner of the state.

But neither did he think of the church as a purely spiritual community, one far removed from any sort of power in society. What he did was to change fundamentally the whole notion of power. The institutional power of the church ought to be exercised through means that are proper to the church, especially through the word that creates a common awareness, and not through politico-ecclesiastical means, always on the lookout for concessions from the state. It ought to be exercised for the good of the people, and not for the good of the institution to the detriment of the people.

This change in the understanding of what power meant was not merely theoretical. It changed the church's base. The church found its place, its home, amidst the people. And it was with the people, not with the state, that the church entered into dialogue. From the people he learned what it was to put one's authority at their service. It was his oft-repeated assertion that the church's authority ought to be at the service of the people, and he put this into practice by bringing the church to those it ought to serve. The church's institutional authority was used not only *for* the people but *with* the people as well. It was no longer exercised from above but from within.

This description of Romero's apostolate as bishop does no more than depict — and, indeed, just as Puebla asked (see 682–84) — the evangelical figure of a pastor, of Jesus. With him, the sheep were safe (John 10:9); his function was to give them life, and life in abundance (John 10:10); he knew his sheep, and his sheep knew him (John 10:14); he was always ready to lay down his life for them (John 10:11).

It is beyond doubt that Romero's faith helped him to make the office of bishop more Christlike. But it is also beyond doubt that his episcopal office helped him to make his faith more real, to make it astoundingly effective. Whatever the theories about the episcopate, Romero demonstrated by his actions that it is possible to live out to the full the Christian understanding of that office. He also demonstrated just how important the office of bishop can be in making the faith effective in Latin America. Romero did not theorize about the various issues currently being debated in the theology of the episcopate. He brought into being a new theology of the episcopate simply by his actions. He did not ignore the traditional characteristics of his office, but in the theology that he lived he made those characteristics more concrete and more complete in a new historical context.

Speaking purely sociologically, one cannot expect many bishops with Romero's humane, Christian qualities to emerge. But speaking theologically we have in him a concrete model of what a bishop, with a gospel faith, ought nowadays to be like, and an example of how important it is for a bishop to make that faith effective for liberation. That is no small merit to his credit.

His Judgment on El Salvador

Romero truly loved his country. In his apostolate as arch-bishop he put that love into deeds. Without wanting to do so, he became a national leader. His influence in El Salvador was first of all in the religious sphere but, as he was well aware, it would also be a direct social influence, and an indirect political influence — though in no way did he directly involve himself in politics.

Romero denounced all that disgraced the country; he pro-claimed tirelessly the need for a new society; he strove to hu-manize the processes of change. To record all the positions he took up, all the work that he did during his three years in office, would be an endless task. Instead I am going to attempt to analyze the Christian principles that lay behind his judgment on the three options with which El Salvador was confronted.

Christian Principles

The principles I refer to arose from Medellín and have been generally accepted in the Latin American church. They have not, however, been accepted in conservative circles, even as broad guidelines.

In my view four fundamental principles guided Romero's judgment:

1. The church is not the same thing as the Kingdom of God; it is the servant of the Kingdom. It ought, therefore, to practice the love and justice that enable the Kingdom to take concrete shape. It ought to be an instrument at the service of the King-dom and in consequence cooperate with those who truly want a more just society, even if they are not explicitly Christians themselves.

2. The poor are those for whom the Kingdom is primarily intended. Not that the Kingdom ought to be constructed for them: they themselves should be the makers of their own des-tiny. It follows that they cannot be denied the major part in any process leading to the establishment of the Kingdom.

3. As the servant of the Kingdom, the church ought also to

promote the values of the members of the Kingdom, both while the new society is being built up and when it is at length achieved.

4. For the church in any way to impede or thwart either the Kingdom of God or the members of the Kingdom is sinful. This is true both at the personal and at the structural level, and this sin has degrees of wickedness that will be important to consider when making judgments about de facto situations and courses of action.

These principles can be clearly seen at work in all that Romero did, but he was also well aware that, because they are *general* principles, they have to be put into practice in accordance with the signs of the times. The need to make these principles concrete was an important part of his understanding of them. He therefore gave new importance to a much-neglected canon of pneumatology—that is to say, to the affirmation that the Spirit is constantly at work in history.

In order to understand the judgments that Archbishop Romero made about El Salvador, one has to bear in mind the way in which some key principles were put into practice. Of these principles the following seem to be the most significant:

1. Romero concretized the concept of "the poor." Although recognizing the profound truth in the gospel presentation of spiritual poverty, he went beyond it. In accord with Puebla (31–39), he described poverty as it is today in El Salvador. But more than that, he saw in every poor person not just an isolated individual but the "masses." To speak of the poor was to speak of *the* problem in El Salvador. He regarded the masses not just as a sum of individuals but as a collectivity, as a people—however much one would have to nuance this statement sociologically. He saw in this collectivity a social grouping utterly opposed to the ruling group—though as a pastor he was not concerned to analyze the class nature of those groups. In this way he advanced beyond the usual view of a poor person as a peaceable individual who is, at most, the object of an ethical demand upon us. He saw the poor as a collectivity, the very existence of which—and increasingly so as it grows in self-understanding—signals social conflict.

2. Romero concretized what it meant to say that the people

ought to be the agent of its own destiny and not simply the beneficiary of real or feigned charity. Hence he understood the logic of moving from "people" to "organized people." He defended, as a Christian principle, the right of a people to organize itself. Though as a pastor he imposed on no one the obligation of joining an organization, he positively encouraged them to do so, though without going so far as to point out which particular organization came closest to fulfilling the ideal of an organized people.

He grew in understanding of the purpose that lay behind a people's banding together. From the very beginning he saw the legitimacy of a people's organizing itself to fight for, or to defend, its rights. But he also came to understand, especially in the last months of his life, the importance of a people's organizing itself so as to take over, or to be substantially represented in, political power. He recognized that no political program will successfully benefit the majority of a people unless its own organizations play a major part in the political life of the country.

3. In his promotion of a more just society he introduced the novel idea of the "viability" of theory and practice. The viability of theory prompted him to analyze different political options. He asked himself which was the likeliest to bring about a society most closely resembling the Kingdom of God. As a pastor he was concerned with the viability of practice. It was not as a political analyst but as a pastor that he drew attention to the ways that, in his view, were most likely to bring the new society into being. Naturally, there is a tension between the viability of theory and the viability of practice, and Romero understood this. But it is important to emphasize once again that in making actual the Kingdom of God he did not concern himself simply with proclaiming it. He thought hard about the viable ways of building the Kingdom in El Salvador.

When rooting these Christian judgmental principles in his particular time and place, Romero was deepening his understanding of them. At times he changed his mind. His pastoral letters and his Sunday homilies recount the story of this process. It is important to draw attention to the fact that this rooting in history, with all its complexity and its nuances, even with its changes, had a definite, historical direction. This has to be said because, and especially since his death, he has frequently been presented as someone who was a defender of human rights in the abstract, who loved peace and justice, but who lacked any clear, practical, historical commitment. It is true that he touched on a whole variety of different issues, and that he did so in such changing circumstances that one can always find a quotation to support one's own views. It is possible to play off what he said on different occasions in such a way as to suggest that, having said everything, in the end Romero had said nothing. But that was never his intention, nor is it an objective picture of what happened.

Romero did not apply his general Christian principles to the history of his own time simply on the basis of purely abstract theological reasoning. Nor did he base himself on the evolving magisterium of the church on socio-political matters, though undoubtedly both the theology and social teaching helped him. The principle behind his process of adaptation was the very history of his country or, to put it theologically, the manifestation of the Spirit in that history. That is why his thinking went along fairly clear-cut lines as he himself progressed in discovering, in quite practical terms, the will of God for El Salvador.

As a way of checking on the validity of the development and the direction of his social thinking one ought not to ignore the reaction, both at home and abroad, to his active involvement: the public image that the people as a whole and different social groups had of him. That reaction, that image, are proof enough that his activities led in a definite direction, that his commitment was not merely to the universal values of peace, love, justice, and human rights, but to programs that would best guarantee those values.

The Three Political Options

On the basis of the criteria already cited, their realization and development, Romero passed judgment on the three options confronting El Salvador. He called them the proposals or programs of the oligarchy, of the governing junta, and of the people.

He condemned the policy of the oligarchy—the infamous

fourteen families, and their allies, that effectively control the destiny of El Salvador—because it was clearly evil. "When all is said and done, the right wing stands for social injustice. There is no justification for maintaining a right-wing stance," he told *El Diario de Caracas*.[2] His Fourth Pastoral Letter denounced its policies as idolatrous—based upon mendacity. It served an idol that, in order to survive, needed more and more victims. It was unacceptable both to Christianity and to history. After fifty years of misery the masses, with their growing political awareness, could tolerate it no longer.

Romero's judgment on the policy of the governing junta changed between the first and second junta. He was hopeful about the first one. He did not give it his blessing, nor did he give it unconditional support—though he gave it critical support. He saw that there was a chance of implementing the Christian principles outlined above. There were grounds for hope in the fact that the coup had been bloodless, in the honesty and the good intentions of many of the new leaders, and in the promises of radical reform and of dialogue with the popular organizations.

But none of this became viable. Repression continued. No one was any the clearer about the fate of all those who had vanished for political reasons. Those who were responsible were not brought to trial—something that Romero regarded as a requirement of simple justice and as a sign that there had been a break with the past. Reforms could not be carried out. There were large-scale resignations by conscientious members of the government, and this convinced him that the policy of the junta would not work.

The second junta had a clearer political program. Romero defined it as "reforms with the big stick"—reforms accompanied by repression. With increased vigor he condemned, as he had always done, the repression of the people. It had become much worse, both in terms of the number of victims involved and the degree of cruelty with which it was carried out. He condemned the final aim of the repression: the destruction of the popular organizations. It was the aim of a faction in the government that, Romero said, acted like a parallel government. He was brought to the point where, with unequalled passion, he called upon the soldiers and other members of the security forces not to obey unjust orders. These were the last words of his last complete sermon:

> In the name of God, then, and in the name of this suffering people, whose screams and cries mount to heaven, and daily grow louder, I beg you, I entreat you, I order you in the name of God: Stop the repression! [March 23, 1980].[3]

Because of the repression he became suspicious of the agrarian reform that was announced. Though he stressed its necessity, he foresaw its impossibility because, as Scripture says, land stained with blood will not bear fruit (Gen. 4:12). Agrarian reform ought not to be granted to the people as if it were a gift. It is something they have earned by all the blood they have paid for it. Even in the days of the first junta Romero laid down the real significance that agrarian reform ought to have but that he did not see when it first began to be implemented:

> Agrarian reform should not be undertaken simply so as to find a way of salvaging the capitalist economic system, and allowing it to go on developing in such a way that wealth is accumulated and concentrated in the hands of a few, whether they be of the industrial, commercial, or banking sectors of society. Nor should it be done so as to silence the *campesinos,* to prevent them from organizing themselves and so increasing their political, economic, and social involvement. Agrarian reform ought not to make the *campesinos* dependent upon the state. It ought to leave them free in their relationship with the state [December 16, 1979].

He drew the consequences of his denunciation of this political program. He asked the Christian Democrats to rethink their position in the government. Just five days before his death he gave the following answer to a journalist who was questioning him about it:

> I am no expert in politics. I can only repeat what I have heard from prominent analysts. Even though it is true they

have the good intention of carrying through structural reforms, the Christian Democrats run a grave risk in being
part of a government that is engaged in such fearful repression. In this way the Christian Democratic Party is becoming an accomplice in the annihilation of the people. I want
to tell you journalists to be clear and objective in your
reporting of what is going on in El Salvador. I have often
heard it said by persons who live abroad and do not understand what is going on here: "The Christian Democrats
are there; they are carrying out reforms; what more do you
want? Why do you complain?" So it should be made clear
that yes, there is the Christian Democratic Party, and yes,
there are reforms. But the only thing the people know is
terrible repression [interview in *El Diario de Caracas*].

It is in this context that one has to understand his letter to
President Carter. The United States has no right to intervene
in El Salvador, no right to lend support to a policy that is said
to be opposed to the oligarchy but in reality is opposed to the
interests of the people, no right to provide military support just
as repression grows in intensity (see the homily of February 17,
1980).

Romero certainly had no objections to a reform policy in
itself, provided it really opened the way to reforms, and to the
integration of the people and their organizations in the political
process. But he did not regard the superficial reform policy of
the junta as one that was viable for Christians. Nor did he believe that the people would support it in the long run.

Over his three-year period as archbishop, Romero's judgment
on the people's self-liberation evolved to the point where, in the
last three months of his life, he came to think of it as the historical force that offered most hope. He thought this for two
reasons: the others would not work, and the popular organizations, which were the main protagonists of the people's interests,
had gone through a long process to reach maturity.

It has already been pointed out that the reality of the poor
and their being the "agents of their own destinies" had brought
Romero face to face with the situation of the popular organizations. He gave over a large part of his Third and Fourth Pas-

toral Letters to this topic. Here I want to sum up briefly his attitude to the popular organizations, what he criticized in them, what the criticism meant, his support for them, and the hopes that they engendered in him. For though the general tendency of his attitude was clear, it was complex and nuanced.

Romero criticized everything he saw as wrong-headed or dangerous in the popular organizations, both from a Christian and from an ordinary human point of view. He criticized all that he regarded as dehumanizing in them, either in their effect on their members or in their effect on the country. He warned them severely against the danger of thinking that the point of view of their own organization was the only possible one, and against the danger of reductionism: seeing everything from a political angle and neglecting other areas of life. He accused them of being dogmatic and sectarian, of being divided among themselves, of being separated from other political groups and even from the people itself. He denounced some of their actions as being disproportionately violent. On occasion he even denounced their violence as little different from terrorism — though he did not think it so typical of the popular organizations as it was of the politico-military groups. He accused them of claiming to be more representative of the people than they actually were, of sometimes failing to take account of the religious feelings of the people and their most cherished expressions of those feelings. In some extreme cases, he said, they wanted to manipulate or even to destroy the people's Christian faith.

It is important to make clear what his criticism meant. His love for the truth moved him to denounce whatever he saw to be mistaken, though he perfectly well understood that so vast a social phenomenon as the popular organizations would be bound to make some mistakes. His criticism of them was different from that directed against the other two options for liberation of the masses. He criticized the popular organizations because he had hopes for them. He wanted them to improve, to grow, and to serve the people better. He denounced the absolutization of politics because "one could, for all practical purposes, ignore all other real problems or mistake the basic ideological criteria" (Fourth Pastoral Letter). He attacked sectarianism because "it changed what was a likely force for the people's good into an obstacle impeding radical social change" (ibid.). He attacked disparagement of the Christian faith because it showed no respect for the reality of the faith among the people, and because "it would be a mistake to place in opposition to each other the driving force within the organizations and the driving force within the church" (ibid.).

On the other hand, in the popular organizations Romero saw a range of humane, Christian values that were beneficial for the country as a whole and that the church would do well to learn. He admired the justice of their struggle, the moral weight of their cause, the generosity and strength of their commitment, and their readiness to devote their lives and their possessions to the people. These qualities were more in evidence among the popular organizations than they were in other political groups. And he admired their values although he knew that, alongside Christians, there were also nonbelievers in the popular organizations. This was no reason for him not to give the organizations his admiration and support. He was convinced that "even outside the church's precincts, Christ's redemption has great power, and peoples struggling for freedom, even though they are not Christian, are inspired by the Spirit of Jesus" (Third Pastoral Letter).

Toward the end of his life, though he kept up his criticism, he came to realize that the popular organizations had entered upon a stage that, taken all in all, he regarded positively. He had called for unity, and for the overcoming of sectarianism. With the creation of the CRM (Coordinadora Revolucionaria de Masas—Mass Revolutionary Coordinating Committee) and its opening up to other social and politically democratic forces, these ends seemed about to be attained. Romero did not live to hear of the formation of the FDR (Frente Democrático Revolucionario—Democratic Revolutionary Front) on April 2, 1980. But he knew of the first steps that were being taken, and was delighted by them. In fact, through the good offices of the archdiocesan Legal Aid Bureau he was, in a manner of speaking, to be found in the Halt to Repression document signed by several of the democratic groupings. The formation of a democratic front had been sought by several democratic groups. But it was made possible by the openness of the CRM and its desire to weld together other forces in society on behalf of the popular program.

He was also pleased when the CRM presented a unified platform, because that fact presupposed a wholly new form of unity. It was a response to his explicit request that the people know along which paths the CRM intended to lead the country. We cannot know what he would have thought about the content of the policy adopted by the CRM. The only thing we have is his reply, given in the interview already quoted, when he was asked about it: "I know of it, and I accept it as a basis for discussion among the people. There has to be a readiness to receive criticism and comment from every sector, so that it can be the people itself that forges the government it desires."

Finally, in the last stage of the CRM, he was anxious, and he insisted that the new program should respect the people's human and religious values. The presence of many Christians in the popular organizations and the readiness of the organizations and the CRM to engage in dialogue with the church and other Christian institutions appeared to him to give some guarantees of such respect. He insisted on this partly because it was his clear duty as archbishop to do so, and partly from his awareness of what it means to be a Salvadoran. The popular program ought to find a place for Christianity because Christianity is an important part of the people's life.

Romero showed that he had great hopes for the popular program while it was being drawn up. He did not idealize it, however. He made suggestions for improving it, and kept demanding that it display greater maturity. From his homily of January 20, 1980, onward, he repeatedly referred to his hope in it. Not that he identified himself with it, or with any other current political program. Taking politics in the strict sense of the word, he could not do so, because of his position as archbishop. In any case he believed that it would be more fruitful for the development of the country if he kept a certain distance. But there is no doubt at all that he saw in the popular program the best, and the most workable, translation into political terms of the option for the poor that he so radically defended in pastoral terms.

Hence it would be a mistake to present Archbishop Romero as a man of the center, keeping himself equidistant from the left and the right. It would be a mistake because it would imply that he acted on the *negative* principle of avoiding extremes. In fact he acted out of *positive* principles, asking himself what would lead to deeper truth, greater justice, stronger possibilities for peace. The popular program, he found, had these in greater abundance and with greater potential. He wanted to avoid the trap that the very terminology "right," and "left," and "center," offers, as if it were the job of an archbishop to choose the center *ex officio*. In the interview quoted above he was asked what the "left" meant for him. He replied, "I don't call them the forces of the left but the forces of the people. . . . What they call 'the left' is the people. It is the organization of the people, . . . and their demands are the demands of the people." Romero did not choose not to choose—which, in effect, is what to be "of the center" means. He made a choice: he opted for the people.

The Church's Role in the Salvadoran Crisis

Romero saw clearly that El Salvador was passing through a period of change, a period of agitation giving rise to conflict. In the conflict the protagonists of each of the three national options were trying to push their own program into the leading position. He also saw clearly that it was the church's duty to pass judgment not only on political programs, but also on the process of change itself. It ought to enter into it, so as to humanize it along Christian lines.

He took up a stance on the conflict inherent in the process and on violence. He had to decide whether or not violence was legitimate and how to humanize it wherever possible.

In making his fundamental ethical judgment on violence, Romero distinguished between the violence of provocation and the violence of response. He recalled the traditional doctrine of proportionate violence in legitimate self-defense, and expounded the degrees of violence as presented by Medellín.

Medellín clearly condemned the violence of provocation that springs from institutionalized injustice. It becomes institutionalized violence or, in the particular case of El Salvador, general repression. From this point of view he saw a violent response as legitimate and just. In the constitutions of the popular organizations he saw the first response to structural injustice. Their means were not essentially violent ones. They were rather those of social pressure. But when the popular organizations were attacked for making use of social pressure, then they had a right to defend themselves. This is how he put it in a carefully phrased paragraph in his Fourth Pastoral Letter:

> We are also aware that great numbers of *campesinos,* workers, slum dwellers, and others who have organized themselves to defend their rights and to promote legitimate changes in social structures are simply regarded as "terrorists" and "subversives." They are arrested, tortured, they disappear, they are killed without any concern for the law or for those legal institutions that are there to protect them. They have no chance to defend themselves or to prove their innocence. Confronted by this harmful and unjust situation they have frequently been forced to defend themselves, even to the point of having recourse to violence. And lately the response to this has been the arbitrary violence of the state.

Within the context of legitimate self-defense, Romero condemned what was out of proportion. He also condemned terrorist violence—more typical of paramilitary political groups than of the popular organizations. Though at times it may be difficult to distinguish between legitimate armed violence and out-and-out terrorism, he took great care to analyze situations and to condemn terrorism.

That is why he did not simply condemn violence "wheresoever it may come from." In a manner that is rarely to be found in the pronouncements of bishops he said, "The church cannot simply assert that it condemns all forms of violence" (Fourth Pastoral Letter). He tried to analyze each case carefully and to judge in accordance with the de facto circumstances.

But Romero was not content simply to judge the legitimacy or illegitimacy of acts of violence. He also attempted to humanize courses of action that involved violence. Though there were cases when violence might be *just,* Romero tried to make it *good* as well. He put Salvadorans on their guard against those unfortunate by-products of violence that can occur even when violence is legitimate. He insisted on the need to overcome hate, to overcome the instinct for vengeance, the temptation to make violence the chief and the basic means of achieving one's ends. He energetically condemned what he called the mysticism of violence.

More positively, he promoted the use and effectiveness of peaceful means even when violence might be necessary to some extent. Romero was not a pacifist pure and simple. By nature he was a peaceful man. As archbishop he was a peacemaker. So as to humanize even the violence that was legitimate, he repeatedly drew attention to all the other elements that had to be employed in building up peace: justice, dialogue, truth, magnanimity.

Romero was also aware of the possibility of armed insurrection. He dwelt on the subject in his pastoral letter, and he often alluded to it in his final homilies. Conscious of the influence he had in society at large, he tried by his actions to prevent the growth of a war mentality, though he had to recognize that there were already so many dead that the situation resembled an undeclared war. But he was always trying to avoid it, trying to find other means of bringing about radical changes. Recent events raised in him the hope that the popular cause might gather so much impetus, and bring together so many different sectors of society, that change might be the most peaceful, and the least violent, possible. Nonetheless he did not exclude the possibility of insurrection. He fought for reconciliation until the last, seeing it as one of his most important tasks. But when asked, during the interview cited above, what would happen should reconciliation prove impossible, he replied laconically, "Well then, the church allows for insurrection when all other peaceful means have been exhausted."

Romero thought the popular program was the best one for the people of El Salvador, for it seemed that it was the policy best able to guarantee enduring structures of justice. But conscious of his role as a churchman, he insisted upon, and worked for, the ideal that it be achieved with what was best from among the people of El Salvador, and that it should incorporate the values of the people of El Salvador. Putting it theologically, he was concerned both for the Kingdom of God, and for the men and women of that Kingdom. With a rare and deep understanding, he pleaded for a conversion of structures and a conversion of hearts.

It was evident that his interest was in persons and not simply in structures when he spoke as a Christian to Christians, and also when he spoke to the people of El Salvador as a whole. In the first instance he emphasized the explicit values of Christianity: faith in God, prayer, openness to Christ—realities that, for him, made men and women human. In the second case he promoted authentic Christian values, though they were not put forward as Christian, for the birth of a new people in El Salvador.

This new people ought already to be in the making, even in the present conflict, as we have seen. It ought to be looked on as the beginning of the future of a new society. Though we do not know what Romero thought of the manifesto of the CRM, I believe that he would have insisted upon analyzing the human, the cultural, the spiritual, and the Christian values of the people of El Salvador, and would have regarded this as the proper role for the church to play. He would have understood that a political manifesto is customarily more concerned with an analysis of a country's structural problems, but he would have remarked that, although new structures no doubt help, they cannot automatically resolve human problems. He recognized that structures do not change merely out of a people's goodness of heart, but neither will hearts change simply because of better structures. In this sense he stressed that the popular cause ought to acknowledge and enhance all that is best in the people of El Salvador, in their cultural inheritance and religious values.

Romero saw toward the end that to humanize this liberative process the church must be present within it. It ought not ignore it or judge it merely from the outside, despite all the conflict and ambiguity that are inherent in any such process. He himself was present within it. This is very clear both from his range of activities as archbishop and from all those innumerable particular occasions when he took it upon himself to dialogue with, to mediate on behalf of, and to stand alongside the people. It is also clear that he wanted all Christians, including the clergy, to be involved in the process and not try to avoid the most difficult aspect of it — that of associating themselves with politically committed Christians.

He believed that the church ought to be present in the process in a way specifically in accord with its nature. That is to say, the church ought to be an evangelical force that becomes a social force, directly, and a political force, indirectly. He believed this ought to happen for the good of the process and for the church's support to be more effective. Although, in the short term, it might seem that the church would be less effective if it stayed close to its own specific vocation in its involvement, Romero was convinced, and history has borne him out, that if it did so the church's influence would be greater and more humanizing in the long term.

He did not believe that it was the church's proper role to direct the process. The church should make its presence felt in the manner of leaven. De jure it was not the church's task to undertake political leadership, though he himself gave far-reaching social leadership. And de facto he knew that among the leaders in the process there were many Christians, as well as unbelievers. The church's presence ought not to come about by way of purely political means, but rather through the objective strength of its truth, its cogency, and its influence in society.

Romero regarded the church's presence in the process as being of the highest importance both for the process itself and for the future of the church. If it were not to be present then it would afterward be displaced by those — *ex hypothesi* outside the church — who had spent their blood and their lives for the popular cause. He did not share the common belief that the church has only an abstract right to speak to, and have an influence upon, society. A church that *ex hypothesi* has abandoned the people in its forward march cannot afterward try to put itself in the vanguard of the people.

Finally, Romero wanted the church to be present in the process for a simple and profoundly Christian reason: the incarnation. The first truth one says of Christ ought also be said of the church. But not infrequently, when the church is faced by new developments that involve conflict and ambiguity, it is tempted to stand to one side, to judge developments from the outside.

The transcendence of the faith is commonly cited in defense of this attitude.

Romero believed profoundly in the transcendence of faith. But he believed in it in a Christian manner. He believed that the church ought to "take flesh" in the world as it really is. It ought to maintain the transcendence of the faith not by alienating itself from, but by submerging itself in, particular situations, judging them, learning from them, always humanizing them, always trying to eliminate what is dehumanizing. The "more" that rises from the depths of humanity is that which directs the church toward the authentic transcendence of God.

It was, hence, because of the faith that Romero believed that the church ought always to make itself present, and to do so in a manner proper to the church. If the church fails to be present in current developments, then the church will simply stop being the Christian church, the church of Jesus, the church that believes in God.

Let us end where we began. If Archbishop Romero played a leading role in the church and in society, it was because of his profound faith in the God of Jesus. That is why he was such a spiritual, such a religious, man, such a close follower of Jesus. It was precisely because of these things that he knew how to renew the life of the church, and how to guide the nation along the road of liberation.

His martyrdom simply confirmed the truth of his life and his cause. His faith in God led him to foresee his martyrdom. He looked upon it as the final service he could render to the church and to his country. This is what he said in his last interview, one that he gave to *Excelsior* (Mexico City) just two weeks before his death:

> I have frequently been threatened with death. I must say that, as a Christian, I do not believe in death but in the resurrection. If they kill me, I shall rise again in the Salvadoran people. I am not boasting; I say it with the greatest humility.
>
> As a pastor I am bound by a divine command to give my life for those whom I love, and that includes all Salvadorans, even those who are going to kill me. If they

manage to carry out their threats, I shall be offering my blood for the redemption and resurrection of El Salvador.

Martyrdom is a grace from God that I do not believe I have earned. But if God accepts the sacrifice of my life, then may my blood be the seed of liberty, and a sign of the hope that will soon become a reality.

May my death, if it is accepted by God, be for the liberation of my people, and as a witness of hope in what is to come. You can tell them, if they succeed in killing me, that I pardon them, and I bless those who may carry out the killing.

But I wish that they could realize that they are wasting their time. A bishop will die, but the church of God—the people—will never die.

Chapter 3

Archbishop Romero: True Prophet*

In chapter 2, I sought to present a theological analysis of Archbishop Romero's person and activity in general. Now I shall attempt to analyze one of the most salient dimensions of that activity: his propheticism. To be sure, this dimension of his apostolic labors and personal existence is not the only aspect of those labors and that existence. Besides being a prophet, Archbishop Romero was a shepherd, a teacher, and an administrator, as indeed a bishop must be.[4] But unless we consider his prophetic word, and consider it in such a way as to recognize its central position in his life and work, we must surely fall short of an adequate comprehension of the basic element of both his mission and his martyrdom. Furthermore, it is his prophetic word that has aroused the most determined attempts to silence him posthumously, just as it has been that word that has been the object of such energetic attempts at appropriation on the part of political systems and certain ecclesiastical curias. But it is precisely owing to Archbishop Romero's physical absence from our midst today that his prophetic word has attained its just dimensions — extraordinary dimensions indeed.

When I speak of Archbishop Romero's word as "prophetic," I am using this adjective in its most rigorous, technical meaning. Archbishop Romero was a prophet not only in that contemporary acceptation of the term according to which we can be said

*Originally published as "Monseñor Romero: Profeta de El Salvador," *Estudios Centroamericanos,* October-November 1980, pp. 1001–34.

to have a "prophetic church," for example, but even in the strict sense in which the great prophets of Israel, whose line culminated in John the Baptist and Jesus of Nazareth, were prophets. "I doubt that there have been more than a dozen authentic prophets, in the biblical sense, in the course of history—Amos, Isaiah, and so on.... You have had the privilege of knowing such a prophet," I have been told by one of the world's foremost experts on the prophets of Israel. He was speaking of Archbishop Romero.

The praise lavished on dead heroes can sometimes be exaggerated and rhetorical. My designation of Archbishop Romero as a prophet is nothing of the kind. It is intended, and is to be understood, in the strictest, most profound theological sense. The category of propheticism is as basic and as essential for Christian faith today as it was basic and essential for the people of Israel in the time of Amos, Isaiah, or Jeremiah. A theological consideration of Archbishop Romero's propheticism, then, will mean an in-depth investigation of a current, concrete, and extraordinary example of one of the fundamental ways in which God manifests the divine will with regard to history, and conversely, one of the fundamental ways in which the agents of history may respond, and correspond, to this divine will.

The method I propose to follow will begin with a general presentation of the prophetic view of the reality of God, God's word, and the divine will for history. This first step will necessarily be very brief and somewhat abstract. But we shall need an understanding of the nature of prophecy in the biblical tradition in order to pursue my investigation of Archbishop Romero's prophetic word—the question to which I shall devote the greater part of the present chapter. In this latter stage of my considerations I shall cite Archbishop Romero extensively—not, however, for the purpose of compiling an anthology, but in order to demonstrate the fact and meaning of his propheticism, and the organization of the citations will be determined by this end.

Concretely, I shall organize Archbishop Romero's prophetic word around the three following points:

1. The Historical Dimension of the Prophetic Word: the concrete content of God's word in its exposé and denunciation of society's sinfulness and of those responsible for it, its announcement of the punishment to be meted out to the latter, its demand for their conversion, and its proclamation of hope for the future.

2. *The Theological Dimension of the Prophetic Word:* the ultimate origin of this word, and its formal characteristics precisely as the word of God, in virtue of which it judges not only history, but the church.

3. *The Eschatological Dimension of the Prophetic Word:* the inevitable fate of this word and its human vehicle, and the survival of this word after the disappearance of the prophet.

Historical Dimension of the Prophetic Word

"With Archbishop Romero, God has visited El Salvador" (Ignacio Ellacuría). This assertion is true in a number of ways. And it is true especially because in Archbishop Romero our country has seen the mercy, love, and justice of God. For the moment, however, let us analyze the truth of this statement from the perspective of the prophetic word, along the lines of the Profession of Faith we recite at the eucharist: "We believe in the Holy Spirit. . . . He has spoken through the prophets." God becomes present in the proclamation of the divine will through the mouth of the prophets.

The first basic characteristic of the prophet is that a prophet proclaims the will of God, and proclaims it directly in its bearing on historical reality, in all of the social, economic, political, and cultural complexity of the latter. True, the prophet is a religious figure. But the content of the prophetic message does not bear directly on the religious scene. It bears on the totality of secular, worldly history. The prophetic word bears on the life and death of men and women, on the relations of justice or injustice generated among them, on oppression and liberation. The strictly religious element of concrete life, while requiring explicitation, is not presented in authentic prophecy as an autonomous element parallel to the historical. Rather, for the prophets, religion is simply the way in which people live historical reality in ultimacy and according to God.

As we see, then, what today is called "involvement in politics" — usually by way of indictment — is essential to propheticism. Involvement in politics is not merely incidental —

something that ought to occur only "under special circumstances." The political, the economic, and the social are consubstantial with history, and thus constitute the object of God's prophetic will. This was altogether evident to the prophets, who offered no apologia, unlike the church today which must still offer an apologia if it wishes to speak its mind on politics or become "involved" in the same. And it was evident to them because the prophetic call itself sends the prophet to proclaim the will of God to the people and the nations. The prophet is not, then, specifically a professional in church affairs. The prophet is a person on the street, the person who judges history from the viewpoint of God.

Archbishop Romero shared this view of prophecy—although, as he was also a hierarch of the church, he also had to emphasize repeatedly, in the face of countless accusations, that the motivation and the formality of his action were religious and not political. Thus he so often repeated: "I must insist that my sermons are not political. Naturally, they deal with the political. They deal with the reality of the lives of the people. But they do so in order to enlighten the people, and to tell them what is the will of God and what is not the will of God" (January 21, 1979).[5] The source and motivation of Archbishop Romero's activity were obviously religious. But the content of this activity, in its quality as prophetic, was just as obviously the historical reality of El Salvador, at all the levels on which human life is expressed. Archbishop Romero proclaimed God's will for the history of our country. He spoke in a religious fashion. That is, he began with God. But he spoke of concrete history, and therefore he also spoke of things secular. And it is this latter that formally constituted him a prophet.

Comprehensive View of Society according to the Prophets

An analysis of the prophets' comprehensive view of society must necessarily be brief, but it is of supreme importance for an understanding of the genesis of one of the fundamental pillars of the faith of Israel—one that Jesus would take up and perfect. It is likewise of supreme importance simply for demonstrating that not only did Archbishop Romero not separate himself from the foundations of faith, but he actually applied these foundations to the present. Of course, like any authentic application of faith in the current day, he was doing a dangerous thing.

1. With the inequitable division of the land in the eighth century B.C., Israel saw the rise of the phenomenon of land monopoly, occasioning a profound social cleavage between those who hoarded the land and those who were dispossessed of it. Amos, the first of the prophets of the era, issued a forthright condemnation. On one side were those who "lying upon beds of ivory . . . eat lambs taken from the flock . . . drink wine from bowls" (Amos 6:4–6). And on the other side were the poor, who were sold for a pair of sandals; the weak, trampled under foot into the dust of the earth; the needy, who were denied all justice (see Amos 2:6–7).

In the face of this novel, scandalous social phenomenon, the prophet's judgment is clear, historically as well as theologically. Historically, society was corrupt: "See the great disorders within her, the oppression in her midst" (Amos 3:9). And this society was so deeply divided and filled with internal hostility that the prophets regarded it as a society in a state of civil war — or of institutionalized violence, as we would say today. And so they used metaphors of war: ". . . Making widows their plunder, and orphans their prey!" (Isa. 10:2). This society, seemingly so at peace, grovels in the abominations of war: plunder and prey.

On the basis of this bedrock historical judgment, the prophets now pronounced their theological judgment: that is, they now pronounced the word of God. The mighty "know not how to do what is right, says the Lord" (Amos 3:10); nor do they lament the disaster of their people (Amos 6:6). God condemns the division of society into the haves and the havenots. And — scandalous novelty, yesterday as today! — God takes sides. When the prophets spoke in God's name, they minced no words. "You" means the hoarders, and "my people" means the dispossessed. "My people" no longer refers to the totality of Israel. Now the people of God are the poor and oppressed, the orphans and the widows. It is of the very nature of God to be partial to the poor.

2. This sort of society is a sin, and in God's eyes this sin is

the *fundamental* sin. This is why, although they saw failings and sins among the poor as well, the prophets concentrated their denunciations on those responsible for this basic sin. From Amos to Jesus, the prophetic word of God regarded the hoarders, the wealthy, as ultimately responsible for sin. But the prophets soon came to realize that other social groups, influential in public life, made common cause with the wealthy: the people's leaders—judges, priests, false prophets, and so on. Hence their vigorous denunciation of these social groups.

The prophets accused these leaders of "pasturing themselves" instead of their flock (Ezek. 34:2)—of not caring for their flock. In fact, in a strikingly harsh metaphor, they denounced them for actually sacrificing the people to their own selfish gain:

> You who tear their skin from them,
> and their flesh from their bones!
> They eat the flesh of my people,
> and flay their skin from them,
> and break their bones.
> They chop them in pieces like flesh in a kettle,
> and like meat in a caldron [Mic. 3:1–3].

They denounced judges, who ought to be the guardians of justice and defend precisely the oppressed. After all, the oppressed had no other recourse against their oppressors. But law and the administration of justice had been converted into exactly the contrary.

> Woe to those who enact unjust statutes
> and who write oppressive decrees,
> Depriving the needy of judgment. . . .
>   [Isa. 10:1–2]

Lawgivers shape their laws to enrich themselves at the cost of the poor, of widows and orphans (Isa. 10:1–4). Judges lose interest in suits brought by the poor because they are not lucrative (Isa. 1:21–26), and even do them positive injustice (Isa. 5:21–23). Law has been converted into a bitter drink, a deadly poison for the poor (Amos 5:7–15, 6:12).

The prophets denounced the politicians of their times, the kings. While the historical books of the Old Testament contain laudatory assessments of various kings, the prophetic books praise the action of one king alone, Josiah. Jeremiah gives the reason: "He did what was right and just.... He dispensed justice to the weak and the poor ..." (Jer. 22:15–16). Of no other king could the prophets assert this.

They denounced false prophets, who molded public opinion for a fee and held sway in the sanctuary, "the king's sanctuary and a royal temple" (Amos 7:13). They denounced shameless public prevaricators:

> Woe to those who call evil good, and good evil,
> who change darkness into light, and light into
> darkness,
> who change bitter into sweet, and sweet into
> bitter! [Isa. 5:20].

They denounced priests, and those in charge of worship. These functionaries committed a double sin. First, they made use of worship to enrich themselves, actually rejoicing in sin because of the economic benefits they reaped from sacrifices of atonement. "With you is my grievance, O priests! ... They feed on the sin of my people, and are greedy for their guilt" (Hos. 4:4,8). And they used worship to mask over the real sin of society. Hence the terrible, reiterated prophetic words: "Hear the word of the Lord.... I have had enough of whole-burnt rams and fat of fatlings.... Bring no more worthless offerings. ... Your hands are full of blood! ... Make justice your aim: redress the wronged" (Isa. 1:10,11,13,15,17).

Together with their denunciations of their fellow citizens for their sinful society, the prophets also pronounced terrible anathemas against foreign oppressors, the invading empires of the time. The prophets regarded foreign powers in various lights, according to circumstances, but their definitive word on imperialism was clear:

> Because you despoiled many peoples
> all the rest of the nations shall despoil you;

> because of men's blood shed,
> and violence done to the land, to the city and
>   to all who dwell in it [Hab. 2:8].

It is important to notice that the prophets' denunciation of various leaders and social groups had but one ultimate criterion: Who oppresses the people? Hence the prophets' forthright partiality. Today they would be accused of precipitancy, of bias and demagoguery. But the root of their partiality is God. Confronted with society's fundamental sin, God refers to the victims of this sin as "my people," and takes their side against all who oppress them.

3. The prophets were not satisfied with a simple denunciation of society's sin, however harsh that denunciation. They proclaimed God's reaction to this sin. God's reaction to the sin of society can be summed up under three points: proclamation of punishment, call for conversion, and word of consolation.

The prophets foretold terrible punishments for Israel as a social totality: deportations, destruction, annihilation. The very temple, regarded by the Israelites as the foundation and guarantee of their reality as a people, would be destroyed. Such punishment was proclaimed, surely, as an explicit intervention on the part of God. But Jeremiah also declared the intrinsic reason for it:

> Two evils have my people done:
> they have forsaken me, the source of living
>   waters;
> They have dug themselves cisterns,
> broken cisterns, that hold no water [Jer. 2:13].

Historically speaking, a society organized on principles of social injustice necessarily and intrinsically brings chastisement upon itself. It bears within itself the seed of its own destruction.

Would Israel escape punishment? Then let this stiff-necked people be converted. And let the conversion consist in the actual correction of its social sin. No other alternatives were offered. "Return, O Israel, to the Lord, your God" (Hos. 14:2), was the theological formulation of a demand for conversion. But as this

God was the God who referred to the poor and oppressed as "my people," conversion to God could only mean conversion to this people. To return to God meant to do justice.

> Hate evil and love good,
>   and let justice prevail at the gate. . . .
> Then let justice surge like water,
>   and goodness like an unfailing stream.
>   [Amos 5:15, 24]

The prophet's ultimate word to the people was one of consolation and hope. Precisely at the sight of sin, God is moved to pity, and remembers the people of the election. "I will not give vent to my blazing anger . . . for I am God and not man . . ." (Hos. 11:9). As a mother cannot forget the child of her womb, so God will remember the chosen people (Isa. 49:5), and promises them a new heaven and a new earth. There peace shall reign, for "they shall beat their swords into plowshares and their spears into pruning hooks" (Isa. 2:4). There solidarity shall reign, for "the wolf shall be a guest of the lamb" (Isa. 11:6). There justice shall reign: "they shall live in the houses they build, and eat the fruit of the vineyards they plant" (Isa. 65:21).

This, in broad strokes, is the prophetic view of the whole of reality, historical and theological alike. I hold that Archbishop Romero shared this view, and that he historicized it in the Salvadoran situation. It is this view, and this historicization, that I propose to analyze in the following pages, with special attention to his prophetic denunciation of the sin of society—the sin that, for him, cried to heaven. Here was a sin that he could never permit himself to reduce to banality, and he struggled with it until he was felled by the assassin's bullet. The words of hope and comfort that Archbishop Romero also pronounced, which I shall present more briefly, ring with all of the credibility bestowed on them by the severity of his denunciation.

Prophetic View of Salvadoran Society

Archbishop Romero shared the basic view of society maintained by biblical propheticism, and concretized it for El Salvador. He saw the ultimate root of our sinful situation in the crying economic inequities prevailing in our land, and he denounced those inequities with all forthrightness, indeed, even more radically than they had been denounced at Puebla.[6] "In El Salvador," he said, "we really have to say that the gap between the many who have nothing, and the few who have everything, is actually widening" (February 18, 1979). This is not a natural situation. It is the product of a particular economic system, which represents the first and basic injustice: "Above all, I denounce the absolutization of wealth. This is the great evil of El Salvador: wealth—private property as an untouchable absolute. And woe to you if you touch this high tension wire! You'll get a bad burn . . ." (August 12, 1979).

This basic injustice is the root of a society radically perverted at every level. Thus Archbishop Romero proclaimed that what we have in our country is "a pseudo-peace, a false order, based on repression and fear" (July 1, 1979). "Theft is rapidly becoming the 'name of the game.' You're stupid if you don't steal" (March 18, 1979). "Peoples are toyed with, elections are toyed with, human dignity is toyed with" (March 11, 1979). We live "in a world of lies. No one believes in anything any more" (March 18, 1979).

This social disorder, expressed at all levels, this *op*pression, is expressed first and foremost at the level of *re*pression—a phenomenon that must have been unknown in Israel, since the prophets never mention it. In El Salvador, however, economic oppression has spawned a deadly repression. The purpose of the latter is precisely the maintenance of the economic oppression. In repression, Archbishop Romero saw the cruelest consequence of oppression, and the clearest expression of social disorder. He described the repression of his country in these pathetic words:

I have the job of picking up the trampled, the corpses, and all that persecution of the church dumps along the road on its way through [June 19, 1977]. I shall never tire of denouncing the outrages of arbitrary arrest, disappearance, and torture [June 24, 1979]. The organized sector of our people continue to be massacred simply for an orderly march in the street to ask for justice and freedom [January 27, 1980]. Violence, murder, torture—torture to the death—mass shootings, the hackings and the stabbings, throwing people away—this is all the empire of hell! [July 1, 1979].

In our situation in El Salvador, the cruelty of this repression became Archbishop Romero's ultimate criterion of truth. In repression, the face of popular oppression acquired its most recognizable traits. Quick, violent death was the clearest expression of the generalized slow death of the people by way of unjust, oppressive structures. In Aguilares he described the situation that had gradually come to be general in El Salvador: "They have transformed a country into a prison and a torture chamber" (June 19, 1977). No one was safe in this land: "Here, speech is no longer permitted. You may keep silence and watch your family be killed, or you may speak out and be killed yourself. What a sad state of affairs!" (June 24, 1979). This is what Archbishop Romero called "the empire of hell."

But Archbishop Romero was not content with denouncing and condemning this situation in generalities. He exposed it in its various specific ramifications. It was all-pervasive, and to those who sought to present a glowing picture of a country where all was well, Archbishop Romero answered—like the prophet Micah before him—that it had all been built with blood. "What good are beautiful highways and airports, all these beautiful skyscrapers, if they are all fashioned of the clotted blood of the poor who will never enjoy them?" (July 15, 1979). To those who gloried in so-called social revolutions, supposedly unequalled in Latin America, Archbishop Romero responded: "This blood, these deaths, touch the very heart of God. No land reform, no bank nationalizations, no other promised measures can be fruitful if it is awash in blood . . ." (March 16, 1980).

This is Archbishop Romero's prophetic view of the country as a whole. The country is writhing in the gravest sin. Some have monopolized the goods of the land by depriving others of them, and to defend these ill-gotten goods they do not hesitate to oppress and repress the people. This and nothing else is the basic sin that Archbishop Romero denounced as a prophet: that a few should oppress and repress the majority of the Salvadoran people, whom God calls "my people."

Denunciation of Those Responsible

Archbishop Romero not only condemned this unjust situation, he condemned those responsible for it. Of course, as the shepherd of his flock, he also denounced the sins of the people. But as a prophet, he denounced those responsible for the fundamental sin. These, just as for the prophets of Israel, were the rich monopolists, and other social groups with any type of power, for they had all placed their power at the service of mighty mammon. Let us examine his denunciation of these various oppressive groups.

1. Idolatry of Mammon: Archbishop Romero realized that the root of the ills of his country was to be sought on the level of economics — that the responsibility was to be laid at the doorstep of an oligarchy of wealth that, being an idol, puts forth every claim to legitimacy, imposing its laws and sacrificing everything to wealth. His overall judgment and his basic denunciation were unambiguous:

> We must go to the root if we want to transform our society. If we want the violence to stop, if we want our whole disease to stop, we have to go the root of the disease. And here is the root: social injustice . . . [September 30, 1979]. Until the idolaters of the things of earth are converted to the one true God, they will continue to be our country's greatest threat [November 4, 1979].

The oligarchs are indeed idolaters, since they endow their wealth with the exclusive attributes of God. "They want their privileges left intact" (November 4, 1979). And they defend these privileges as only a deity is defended. "When the political right sees any threat to its economic privileges, it moves heaven and earth to keep its idol intact" (November 11, 1979), be it by superficially civilized and legal means, or be it by barefaced repression. In his last months especially, Archbishop Romero caught a glimpse of the lengths to which the oligarchy would go in order to "keep its idol intact":

> The oligarchy is desperate now. It is blindly trying to repress the people. . . . The dynamiting of radio station YSAX is fraught with symbolism. What does this act mean? Seeing the danger of losing its complete domination over investment control and agricultural exports, and especially its almost total monopoly of the land, the oligarchy leaps to the defense of its selfish interests. It makes no attempt to defend these interests by argumentation or popular support. It defends them with the only thing it has: the money that enables it to buy weapons and pay mercenaries to massacre the people and stifle all legitimate expression of justice and freedom. . . . This is what sets off all the bombs planted under this symbol and sign. (Yes, I mean the bomb that went off at the University of Central America, too.) This is why they have murdered so many *campesinos,* students, teachers, workers, and other organized persons [February 24, 1980].

Archbishop Romero's judgment of the oligarchy was prophetic indeed. As their pastor, of course, he toiled for their conversion. He never abandoned his pastoral task, never neglected the requests of individual members of the oligarchy, and even intervened in cases where certain members of the oligarchy had been kidnapped. But his prophetic judgment of the oligarchy, who destroyed the work of God and annihilated the people, was severe in the extreme. "What you have, you have stolen. You have stolen from the people, who perish in misery" (March 18, 1979). "They torture, they kill, and they value their capital more highly than human beings" (March 16, 1980). "They manipulate the multitudes with what they have stolen from the starving" (December 16, 1979).

Archbishop Romero called this impenitent oligarchy "Christless Cains" (August 12, 1979), "despised by God because they place more trust in money" (July 10, 1979). And when the oligarchy protested that the church was teaching class struggle, he reminded them that it was they who had started that struggle.

It was they who had built a classist society—it was they who consider the people "second class persons" (July 10, 1979).

2. *Idolatry of Military Power:* Archbishop Romero saw that, in the recent history of our country, the military has been the direct instrument of the oligarchy for maintaining the public order necessary for the oppressive economic system, as also for the repression of the population when it threatens that system. Nevertheless he distinguished between those in command and their subordinates, especially in the army, where Archbishop Romero was very well acquainted with the tragic situation in which the rank and file found themselves. Here were the common people, acting as direct, immediate agents of repression. He also appreciated, in his last months, the sane intentions of the junior officers in the military. But withal he denounced three aspects of the military and the security forces.

First was the servility of the military leaders vis-à-vis the oligarchy, who had made them the "playthings of the everlasting manipulators of what is most sacred in our land" (November 4, 1979). Military leaders were totally vulnerable to seduction "by the pressures of those so stubbornly opposed to change" (December 24, 1979). Their first sin, then, was "their willing instrumentalization by the oligarchy, with its vicious practice of simply managing the army as it pleases to defend its own interests against those of the people" (January 6, 1980).

The second thing he denounced was idolatry of the armed institution. During the time of the first junta, certain junior officers tried to take sides with the people. Archbishop Romero saw the structural difficulty of this option precisely because he understood the spirit of military unity. And so he told these officers, understandingly: "I regret that this unity can be whipped into you, and that you have reason to fear the security forces" (October 28, 1979). Nevertheless he urged the military to place the good of the people above the institution. "It seems to me that there is an exaggerated respect for the military institution as such. This is a kind of idolatry. We must keep in mind, dear soldiers, that every institution, even the military, must be at the service of the people" (January 6, 1980).

Finally, he denounced the repressive acts committed by the security forces, especially, and the internalization of their repressive mentality on the part of their individual members. He denounced their cruelty, and their abdication of human feelings.

"No provocation!" he warned them before the labor conflicts (March 11, 1979). "Why are we returning to military solutions for our rural and industrial labor problems, instead of going ahead with political ones?" (December 24, 1979). Why not use nonlethal methods when you decide to break up a demonstration, as is done in other parts of the world? "Instead, when our security forces break up demonstrations, the streets are strewn with dead and wounded" (November 4, 1979).

Our country's primary recourse to repression for the resolution of conflict has dehumanized many members of the security forces, Archbishop Romero believed. These persons are no longer capable of a response to the deepest, most justified cries of the people. "How our people long for even a notice in the mail, so that they can visit the graves of their disappeared, or give them Christian burial, or perhaps have the faintest glimmer of hope that those for whom they have so long despaired may still be alive!" (October 28, 1979). The voices of the people went unheard, however, and Archbishop Romero roared prophetically against "those who order, those who permit, yes, those who revel in these violent arrests, disappearances, torture, and murders, as if they were at the Roman circus" (November 11, 1979).

But Archbishop Romero felt hope, as well, when he saw the attitude of the junior officers, and especially, he felt compassion for the ordinary soldier: "Most of the military, too, are recruited from among this people of the poor" (January 14, 1979). He never lost hope that some day these soldiers' and junior officers' popular roots might be of great assistance in the renewal of society and the restoration of the common welfare as the social ideal (see the homily of October 28, 1979). In fact, he became the echo of the soldiers' cries—after all, they were themselves of the people—and in one of his homilies he read a letter he had received from them. In it we could see that the sufferings of the soldiers were the same as those of the rest of the people. They ask for better food and clothing. They ask that they not be insulted and humiliated. They ask for better pay than their miserable twenty colons a week. And they ask "that we not be sent out to repress the population" (January 20, 1980). This letter was met with some of the most prolonged applause that Archbishop Romero ever received at a homily. He concluded his homily with the simple, laconic comment: "Light from the lowly!"

Even keeping all of this in account, however, even in view of the fact that the ultimate responsibility for repression did not lie with them, it was against the armed forces and security forces that Archbishop Romero pronounced his most thunderous prophetic denunciation:

> I should like to make a special appeal to the men of the army, and in particular to the soldiers of the National Guard, the police, and the constabulary. Brothers! We are the same people! You are slaying your *campesino* brothers and sisters! When a human being orders you to kill, the law of God must prevail: "You shall not kill!" No soldier is obliged to obey an order in violation of the law of God. No one is bound to obey an immoral law. It is time you recovered your conscience, and obeyed your conscience instead of orders to commit sin. The church is the defender of God's rights, God's law, human dignity, and the worth of persons. It cannot remain silent before such an abomination. We ask the government to consider seriously the fact that reforms are of no use when they are steeped in all this blood.
>
> In the name of God, then, and in the name of this suffering people, whose screams and cries mount to heaven, and daily grow louder, I beg you, I entreat you, I order you in the name of God: Stop the repression! [March 23, 1980].

3. Connivance of the Politicians: Archbishop Romero lived under four different political regimes, and, with the exception of the initial hope stirred by the takeover by the first junta, saw precious little to praise in the way the country was governed. In his three years as our archbishop he served his flock under two types of government: military regimes, and mixed military and civilian regimes. He regarded the first as national security regimes. I cannot analyze all of his denunciations here. Let me simply examine some of the things he had to say about the government of General Romero.

His basic criticism was that General Romero had not carried out urgent structural reforms. Furthermore, the Romero government constantly violated human rights. No legal avenues remained open to workers who wished to voice their protests (March 18, 1979). *Campesinos* were prevented from organizing. Illegal arrests abounded. Peaceful demonstrations were dispersed in a hail of bullets, and actual massacres were perpetrated. Instead of investigating the facts, the government imposed a state of siege and permitted the National Police to publish false information (May 13, 1979). Rightist paramilitary groups acted with complete impunity (July 8, 1979). General Romero publicly denied that there was any persecution of the church at the very moment that his security forces were murdering a fourth priest, and Archbishop Romero publicly branded him a liar for this (January 21, 1979).

The depravity of the regime reached the point that the minister of defense, a military officer, took it upon himself to pass a negative judgment on the pastoral activities of certain nuns, thus earning himself Archbishop Romero's public condemnation (September 16, 1979). In the final weeks of the regime, when a last-ditch effort to stay in power included the call for a "national dialogue," Archbishop Romero exposed the ruse, denying that the government had the courage for either dialogue or change (September 23, 1979).

Obviously General Romero's was a national security regime. Archbishop Romero's reaction was blunt, especially where it was a matter of the government's systematic, hypocritical denial that any repression was under way at all.

> Where are the disappeared? . . . When do the exiles come home? . . . When will there be an end to torture and arbitrary arrest? . . . When will the church have actual freedom, and a sense of security? . . . Where are there any sanctions against the violent acts of the security forces? . . . Where are the legal mechanisms of appeal against the injustice and violence of ORDEN [Democratic Nationalist Organization—a paramilitary organization]? [July 8, 1979].

There was no hope for the conversion of this regime, he said. "They commit errors and refuse to acknowledge them" (May 13, 1979). And he accused it of hypocrisy in appealing to constitutional legality to justify its criminal activities. "What crimes are committed in the name of legality!" he said. "What opportunities to crush the helpless with impunity!" he added, referring to the regime's abuse of the state of siege (June 21, 1979).

He knew how to render his overall judgment in crisp, summary form. "The state has transformed itself into an absolute. It allows no one to think differently from the way it thinks. It is sunk in social injustice" (July 8, 1979). "In the name of national security, individual security is institutionalized" (Fourth Pastoral Letter, no. 48).

With the October 15 coup, the political management of our country underwent a formal change. The faint hope held out on the occasion of the takeover by the second junta quickly vanished. Repression simply continued. The mass rejection of all honest civilian members, and even one military one, when it came to constituting the junta, was a sure sign that everything would remain the same. Now the Christian Democratic Party came to power, taking charge of the "political management" of the country (since the "military management" was still in the same hands). From now on, the politicians would be Christian Democrats. And while Archbishop Romero's words to them at first were not disapproving, but rather accorded them the margin of confidence justified by the facts on their *prima facie* merit, he gradually came to express his suspicion, issue denunciations, and make his exposé.

In the first place, Archbishop Romero was suspicious of the new government's intentions. He was surprised that, what with the wholesale dismissal of the other members of the first junta, the minister of defense stayed on—a person "who, if he were honest, and actually interested in the common good, likewise ought to have resigned" (January 6, 1980). With the Christian Democrats now formally in power, he was surprised that the military accepted the conditions imposed on them, seeing that it was the imposition of these very conditions that had motivated them to overthrow the first junta. And he was surprised and concerned at the continuation of a tragedy that pained him so deeply: "I am surprised and saddened at the continued silence concerning the disappeared. The new accord between the party and the armed forces makes no mention of the fact of the disappeared" (January 13, 1980).

At first these suspicions were no more than that — simply suspicions. But they soon crystallized into the conviction that the Christian Democrats had no intention of actually making any changes for the better. On the contrary, the overall situation of the country was gradually deteriorating. The repression continued, and it would soon be simply impossible to form a government with a genuinely popular base.

No government will ever achieve stability if it promises change and social justice and then has its credibility destroyed by alarming reports such as the ones we receive from all sides, on a daily basis, to the effect that a most cruel repression continues to be the order of the day, culminating in the sheer sacrifice of the people.

We call on the members of the Christian Democratic Party, together with all other members of the current government, to enter into dialogue with the popular organizations, and with the other democratic and progressive organizations or sectors, and study ways to create the broad government proposed by the popular organizations themselves together with certain former officials — a government, then, resting not on the support of the armed forces, as today, but on the majoritarian, organized consent of the people [January 20, 1980].

This denunciation, this warning, and this demand were voiced in the celebrated homily in which Archbishop Romero commented for the first time on the three governmental political projects. Four weeks later his words were more severe: "What we finally see this week is that neither the junta nor the Christian Democrats are governing this country . . ." (February 17, 1980). Far from softening, repression was growing harsher, and Archbishop Romero blamed the government. "Unless the junta and the Christian Democrats mean to become the accomplices of all this abuse of power, all of these criminal activities, they must identify and punish the ones responsible" (ibid.).

If the Christian Democrats could not check repression, Archbishop Romero wondered what their actual role in the government was. And here he saw himself under the obligation of denouncing the Christian Democrats in the roundest terms. They were not governing, he said. Instead, "they are aiding and abetting an international hoax. They are only allowed to have the appearance of governing" (ibid.).

> This is something else that Christian Democracy will have to answer for. Its participation in a government composed of representatives of particular political and economic interests is giving countries like Venezuela and the United States an excuse to support an alternative that holds itself out as antioligarchical, but that in actuality is antipopular [ibid.].

Archbishop Romero drew the ineluctable conclusion with delicacy, but also with forthrightness and firmness, in his solemn challenge to Christian Democrats:

> I ask the Christian Democrats to analyze not only their intentions, which may surely be very good, but also the actual effects of their presence in the government. That presence is actually only a cloak for the repressive character of this regime, especially from the eyes of the world. It is urgent that, as a political force that ought to be at the disposition of our people, you examine the alternative bases for an efficient utilization of this force on behalf of our poor—whether as an isolated, helpless political party in a government under the hegemony of a repressive military, or as one more force in a popular government whose support base is not the ever more corrupt armed forces in power today, but rather the majoritarian concept of our people . . . [ibid.].

In early March the junta published its reform decrees. Archbishop Romero refused to be the victim of any illusions, and analyzed the viability and finality of these decrees. Then he made his judgment on the basis of that analysis. In the course of those same days, one of the members of the junta, a Christian Democrat, resigned, citing as one of the reasons his conviction that "opportunities for reforms that will have the people's support have dwindled to the point of their disappearance for good and all" (March 9, 1980). Thus Archbishop Romero wondered about the meaning of these reforms, which were being vaunted by Christian Democrats as part of their everlasting argument for continuing in power: "What do these reforms mean in a context of the overall governmental project, which includes as one of its essential elements—this is now out in the open, and plain for all to see—the bloody, yes, the lethal repression of anyone who comes out in favor of some other national project? (ibid.).

A week before his murder, Archbishop Romero returned to an analysis of what the government had actually become, and of the actual and concrete possibilities for the behavior of the coalition. He saw persons in the government who did not really wish to solve the country's problems. In an obvious reference to Christian Democrats, he said: "Let them do something with their power, or else let them have the courage to confess that they cannot govern, and to expose those who are doing all this harm to our country . . ." (March 16, 1980).

4. Imperialist Intervention on the Part of the United States: Archbishop Romero did not make North American imperialism a constant theme of his denunciation. The main brunt of his denunciation was borne by Salvadoran nationals, who are immediately responsible for the oppression and repression. At the same time he knew perfectly well that the peoples of the Third World are dependent, and that El Salvador is in the orbit of U.S. imperialism. In function of this basic fact, his general thesis was that the major powers should help the poor countries, should help the poor, the people, in these countries, and should not interfere in their internal affairs.

In his last months, however, with the junta's project enjoying the unconditional support of the United States—the principal element in the project's support base—he also exposed and denounced North American intervention, which motivated him to compose and publicly read his celebrated letter to President Carter.

His broad thesis, which echoed Puebla's terms (see Puebla Final Document, no. 505), was a reaffirmation of people's right to self-determination. Hence he condemned it as "unjust and deplorable that, by reason of interference on the part of foreign powers, the Salvadoran people are frustrated, repressed, and prevented from making autonomous decisions as to the economic and political course our homeland ought to follow" (February 17, 1980). Any help offered to El Salvador "must be given to the Salvadoran people unconditionally, that they may exercise their legitimate right to self-determination . . ." (February 24, 1980).

Archbishop Romero had direct knowledge of the U.S. decision to support the second junta, as it was communicated to him by Special Ambassador William Bowdler himself, with the request—to put it mildly—that the church offer its own support. The same message arrived in President Carter's reply to Archbishop Romero's letter. The new junta offered the best prospects for a solution to El Salvador's problems, Carter wrote (March 16, 1980). Archbishop Romero remained unconvinced. As for Carter's comprehensive appraisal of the second junta, Archbishop Romero responded that this was "itself a matter of a questionable political judgment" (ibid). For his own part, he had already forthrightly asserted that the best prospects, and best-founded hopes, lay in the popular project.

The immediate motivation for Archbishop Romero's denunciation of North American imperialism was actual U.S. intervention in our country's affairs. Under the pretext of aiding the country, the United States provided our government with military support, and even engaged in military intervention, all of which redounded to the more severe repression of the people. This interference thus became the object of Archbishop Romero's prophetic denunciation:

> Can you have already forgotten what the pope asked for the poor countries when he was here recently? We have enough weapons and bullets. We are fed up with weapons and bullets. . . . Our hunger is for justice, food, medicine, education, and effective programs of equitable development. Once we have respect for human rights in this coun-

try, the last thing we shall need is weaponry and the machinery of death ... [October 21, 1979].

North American aid could help only if it actually went to the people, to be applied to projects of justice, and to pressuring the government to halt repression and solve the problem of the disappeared.

If these requirements are not met, any military aid from the United States will only come as reinforcements for the repressors of the people. ... Even tear gas and bullet-proof vests are weapons of oppression in the hands of our government — they keep the government from having any trouble repressing the people! ... [November 4, 1979].

And this is how North American aid was used, whatever U.S. intentions may have been. Over and over again, that country had claimed military aid would force the military and security forces to act more humanely. Archbishop Romero wondered where there was any "guarantee that these forces would long continue to act in the people's behalf ..." (February 24, 1980). And to the repeated North American assertion that its policy was only the defense of human rights, and that this was the only intention of the current intervention, Archbishop Romero responded sternly and ironically: "No doubt. But — as we have always said — a "policy" of human rights may not always coincide with the attitude of the church, which defends human rights not out of policy, but out of religious conviction ..." (March 16, 1980).

Archbishop Romero's conclusion was unambiguous and trenchant. He told President Carter, in no uncertain terms: "Really, if you really wish to defend human rights, stop sending military aid to the Salvadoran government" (February 17, 1980).

5. *Corruption in the Judiciary:* Archbishop Romero discovered that, in our country, both the legislative and the judiciary were only in the service of the powerful, at the expense of the interests of the poor. And so he insisted on the basic principle that law should *actually* function in defense of the poor. It was not enough that it be impartial on its face, while actually functioning

to the benefit of the powerful (see message of January 1, 1978). Thus he denounced laws like those of the Defense and Guarantee of the Public Order, protested the successive state of siege decrees, and criticized the new reform laws.

But he concentrated on corruption in the administration of justice—a daily phenomenon of immediate experience. The failure of his countless petitions that the fate of the arrested and disappeared be revealed, the uselessness of his denunciations of the practical nonexistence of *habeas corpus,* the enormous difficulties he saw confronting a group of honest attorneys who sought to do something about prevailing abuses—Christians or non-Christians, he praised and supported these lawyers publicly—all of this was evidence that the administration of justice in our country was in a most lamentable state. He summed up the state of the law in the country with a superbly insightful expression he had heard from a *campesino:* "Law is like a snake. It only bites you if you're barefoot." In its actual functioning, in its administration, law was not impartial: it was tremendously prejudicial to the poor, the barefoot, who could not defend themselves. And so Archbishop Romero gave his determined support to any institution that defended the poor against the infringement of their rights at the hands of the law. He supported Judicial Advocacy, then, the Human Rights Commission, and the Investigative Commission that looked into cases of the disappeared and political prisoners during the regime of the first junta.

His denunciation of institutionalized illegality came to its most concentrated expression in a famous public altercation with the Supreme Court. In his homily of April 30, 1978, Archbishop Romero had denounced what various attorneys and defenders of popular causes experienced on a daily basis: anomalies in judiciary proceedings, the separation of attorneys from their clients, torture of prisoners, judges who ignored evidence of torture, and "hypocritical judges" (*"que se venden"*). And to these concrete denunciations he added his across-the-board condemnation, in the name of justice, of those ultimately responsible for its administration.

What is the Supreme Court doing? Where is the transcendent role, in a democracy, of this branch of govern-

ment, which ought to be above all other powers, and exact
justice of those who trample it under foot? I think that a
great part of the unhealthy state of our country has its
main key here, in the president and all of the other judges
of the Supreme Court of Justice, who with greater integrity
ought to demand of the courts, of the tribunals, of the
judges, of all the administrators of that sacrosanct word
"justice," that they genuinely be "agents of justice" [April
30, 1978].

Archbishop Romero's other denunciations of the high-rank-
ing bodies of the country, similar to this one in content and
spirit, ordinarily went unanswered. This one, however, received
a response from the Supreme Court, asking him to give "the
names of the 'venal judges' [*jueces venales*'] to which your worthy
person makes reference" (Public Communiqué of May 5, 1978).
The intention was to trap him. Archbishop Romero replied at
length the following Sunday, May 14. The tone of his reply was
courteous, and indeed juridically precise in its terms and argumentation. But the spirit of his homily was prophetical.

He began by correcting the Supreme Court's language. He
had referred not to "venal judges," he explained, but to "hypocritical judges" (*"que se venden"*), and used this fine distinction
in language as a springboard to the substance of what he was
really concerned to say. He explained that he had been "denouncing the more general irregularities that concern the entire
system of the judiciary." He exposed the hypocrisy of the Supreme Court's request, in view of the fact of "known groups of
mothers and families of political prisoners, disappeared, and
exiles, and so many denunciations of public venality that have
been aired in the media, not only at home but abroad." What
was of precise interest to him was to "hear and answer the cry
of our oppressed people," which exists and is real, and to which
the judiciary turns a deaf ear.

Moving on to the basic problem, he listed — with the Consti-
tution of the Republic in hand — all of the violations of the rights
acknowledged therein: the rights of *habeas corpus,* of life, liberty,
and property, of freedom to enter and leave the country, of
addressing petitions, such as for amnesty or for a declaration of

the unconstitutionality of the Law of Defense and Guarantee of the Public Order. He denounced irregularities on the part of public functionaries, such as failure to respect constitutional guarantees concerning arrest, freedom of association, and freedom to strike.

This list of specific violations of civil rights demonstrated "an absolute contempt on the part of the honorable Supreme Court of Justice" with regard to those same civil rights. And his prophetic tones rang:

> This honorable court has not remedied these situations, contrary as they are to the public liberties and human rights whose defense constitutes its highest mission. We declare, then, the basic rights of the men and women of El Salvador to be held in daily contempt, without remedy from any institution by way of a denunciation of these heinous violations, and without any attempt to proceed sincerely and effectively to the correction of corrupt processes.

The judiciary had done nothing to prevent any of these violations of human and civil rights, which are ultimately so much more than the violation of the rights of this or that particular social group, but are violations of the people and the poor as such. And so Archbishop Romero went on the offensive against prevailing illegality, concluding, on one occasion, with these stern, ironic words: "This denunciation is imposed on me by the gospel, for which I am ready to accept arrest and imprisonment, though this be only one more injustice."

6. *Falsification in the Media:* Archbishop Romero lived in an atmosphere in which the word of authority was the vehicle not of truth, but of the lie, and in which that word was simply sold to the highest bidder. To make matters worse, the word of authority was simply spread everywhere by the media. The media did not do justice to the truth. Rather, the silence, manipulation, and tergiversation of the media only furthered the cause of injustice. With remarkable exceptions, this is what Archbishop Romero found and denounced in our land.

Truth is missing from our midst [April 12, 1979]. Too many of us advertise a pen for hire and words for sale [February 18, 1979]. The media are very manipulated, very manipulated [ibid.]. They distort the truth [January 21, 1979]. Do not believe all you read in the papers, see on television, or hear on the radio [February 18, 1979].

Archbishop Romero saw the ultimate reason for this situation in the control of the media, for all practical purposes, by the powerful. "They have the necessary means, and in abundance," he said (January 27, 1980). "They can afford to pay for television and radio time" (October 7, 1979). For the *campesinos,* on the other hand, for the popular organizations, for the church, there was no place in the press, frequently not even in paid advertisements. And if a broadcasting station attempted to speak for the people and the church, it was dynamited.

It was abundantly clear to Archbishop Romero that the media were on the side of the powers that be, and hostile to the people. They manipulated the news as they thought necessary to their interests, even if it meant distorting the truth. "The national press publishes photographs only of armed demonstrations. And where are the pictures of the rightists, and the National Guard, who attacked" the demonstrators? (January 27, 1980).

"I have heard a great many false interpretations of Puebla, as well as of the Holy Father's addresses," he declared (February 18, 1979). The media were particularly obedient to authority, he knew, when it came to propagating libel about the church, while ignoring any criticism of power coming from the church, any attack by the church on the prevailing system:

Who will pay for air time to show this other aspect of the pope's message? . . . How nice it would be if, alongside their self-serving, paid notices accusing priests of taking a position on social matters, they paid for the publication of the pope's addresses at Oaxaca, Monterrey, and Santo Domingo, or the part of his encyclical where the holy father explicitly condemns precisely the abuses that the church, and consequently we priests, are conscience-bound to condemn! . . . [July 22, 1979].

In his unforgettable homily on the occupation of the churches, Archbishop Romero pointed his finger straight at the media for the general misinformation in which the country was awash, and defended the extreme measures the people had had to take to make their own voice heard.

The media, too, are to blame, and very much to blame. There would seem to be no room for these reports in the press. Where are the reports of the abuses inflicted on the *campesinos* up in Arcatao, or Aguilares? The news is distorted. If the abuses they suffer are ever to be known, the victims must be permitted to cry out to the people. Their cry is uttered by their church. The church must understand the fact — not justify it, but understand it — that due to the irresponsibility of the press, the radio, and television, the vehicles on which the great purveyors of lies against and opposition to the people rely, . . . the people must express themselves in desperate ways. They are not even permitted to buy advertising space or air time. The church has experienced the same marginalization as the people. How often we have tried to get something published and have only heard that there was "no available space," or "no timeslots left," because what we had to say would have offended the agents of oppression and repression, whom the media so officiously cultivate! Such broad sectors of the communications media, which ought to be serving truth and freedom, . . . fail to do so [September 2, 1979].

Finally, Archbishop Romero denounced the complicity of the media with processes and activities of repression. After the first junta came to power, Archbishop Romero thought he saw the possibility of honesty and justice in the country, and he addressed the media in the sternest possible tones, demanding serious acts of reparation for all the harm they had done.

The communications media, especially the radio and the daily newspapers, owe an explanation, and restitution, to this people for its demonstrated complicity in murder . . . and the corruption of the previous government. It is not easy to forget the cunning attacks, the ignominious calumnies, the irresponsible accusations, the cowardly insults transmitted by these media against institutions, honorable individuals, faithful workers for the church, yes, and the dignity of this archiepiscopal office. Taking advantage of the corrupt situation for their own gain, the media eagerly undertook the publication of the vociferations of a powerful bourgeois minority concealed in persons, groups, and institutions whose actual identity was all but impossible to detect. It is the duty of the media, in virtue of the nobility of their mission to publish the written and spoken word, to expose those actually responsible for such enormous crimes . . . [October 21, 1979].

Archbishop Romero was particularly resentful of the activity of the media because his own charism and profession were those of the word of truth, and for him the word of truth was the vehicle of a contribution to liberation. And so he praised honest journalists, where he found them, and excoriated the run of the mill, the vast majority, for their vicious dereliction of duty. It was also in terms of the media that he presented his prophetic view of a society divided into "those who have too much voice," and who detested his own, "and those who have none," whose voice he was determined to be (July 29, 1979).

7. *Falsification of Religion:* Archbishop Romero likewise denounced a false religion, and false religious leaders, but with two differences vis-à-vis the prophets of Israel, whose denunciation in this area was less drastic than in others.

The first difference—and a very positive one—is that he saw in the church of the archdiocese a church by and large sincerely dedicated to justice, and persecuted by those responsible for repression. This church was part of the oppressed people, and was not a vehicle of oppression, but on the contrary, was the target of repression. As a pastor and shepherd he reminded everyone that "the church is born of sinners" (December 16, 1979) and that therefore all Christians stand in need of conversion. But at the same time he showed that he was proud of his church, which was at the service of justice.

The second difference is that as our archbishop he was the

shepherd of his flock, and therefore preferred private fraternal correction of his priests and pastoral ministers to their public denunciation in cases in which they had failed in the service of justice. And, again as our archbishop, he belonged to the episcopal body of the country. While well aware of the profound disagreement prevailing between himself and other bishops, and even certain members of the papal curia, whose actions did not appear correct to him, he strove to maintain the delicate bonds of episcopal communion rather than denounce that communion, lest he augment already notorious internal divisions.

However, apart from these differences between Archbishop Romero and the prophets of Israel, our modern prophet analyzed the religious phenomenon, and denounced in it what he saw to be an element of connivance with and responsibility for the sin of society, just as had the prophets of old. First of all, he denounced the maintenance of a traditional religion that ignored the practice of justice:

> I am saddened to think that there are individuals who do not develop. They remember their boarding-school days, and would like a static Christianity, like a museum piece. But this is not what Christianity and the gospel are about [June 21, 1979]. Particular liturgical traditions, clerical and religious dress, and particular ways of praying are human traditions. Let us seek what is more pleasing to God— some greater manifestation of a religion that lives amidst the people. Let us "look after orphans and widows in their distress and keep ourselves unspotted by the world" (see James 1:27). This is true religion [September 2, 1979].

Secondly, he denounced a positively alienating religion, a church devoted to the service of oppression. He openly admitted that there had been such a thing. In the past, the church had been guided by "certain economic interests which it was sinful to serve, and, lamentably, the church served them. The church had failed to tell the truth about these interests when it should have" (December 31, 1978). And the same thing was occurring in the present. "It is a scandal in our midst that there should be persons or institutions in the church who care nothing for the poor and who live according to their caprices" (July 1, 1979). Here again, while he favored ecumenism and actively promoted it, he could not sidestep his responsibility to denounce certain evangelical sects that believe that it is "a betrayal of the gospel to be concerned with things of earth," and are of course richly rewarded by officialdom for their preaching, which so effectively "lulls the people to sleep" (December 9, 1979).

In the third place, he denounced the falsification of worship, especially of the most sacred element of Christian worship, the eucharist, whether by its transformation by some priests into a business, or by its utilization for the justification of oppressive regimes. Once more he minced no words: "The Mass is subjected to the idolatry of money and power" (June 24, 1979).

For Archbishop Romero, the eucharist was the locus of the presence of Christ who died and was raised again—and in the tragic circumstances of our country, the eucharist was the point of convergence where the torture and murder perpetrated in our own day, and a people's hope of liberation, join that Christ (June 21, 1979). This is why it was so repugnant to him that the eucharist should be commercialized. "What a shameful thing, when a religion is transformed into a way of making money! No scandal could be more terrible" (November 11, 1979). "Saying extra Masses just to make money is tantamount to lying. It is infidelity and betrayal, like Judas selling his Lord. And no one could complain of unjust chastisement if the Lord undertook a new cleansing of the temple" (June 24, 1979).

Hence he was also most insistent that worship and its celebrants not make themselves available for anything like the legitimation of injustice and repression, or connivance with those responsible for such abuses. And so he refused to schedule government Masses, Pope Days, or Te Deums, and refused to attend political or military ceremonies, which certain other bishops and priests continued to attend. Hence also he denounced the politicization of certain priests who would bestow their automatic, blanket approval on whatever the government happened to be doing (or omitting to do). "Yes, there are many priests in politics. But their politics is one of toadying to officialdom—even of being cardcarrying members of ORDEN..." (January 7, 1979). Without naming names—the people knew whom he meant—he denounced the sin of placing Christian worship at the service of the mighty:

> The Mass is subjected to the idolatry of money and power when it is used to condone sinful situations—when it is utilized to try to show the people that there is no discord between the government and the church. The Mass becomes incidental; the important thing is to get your name in the paper, to be known as a reliable political toady. How we have profaned the eucharist! [June 24, 1979].

As shepherd and pastor of his people, Archbishop Romero demanded a correct practice of religion on the part of all: he denounced all sins against religion committed *despite* a correctly ordered religion. But as a prophet he denounced sin committed *in the name of* religion. He denounced a religion transformed into a vehicle of sin; or a religion that ignored the essential Christian demands of justice, and ignored them on principle; or, worst of all, a religion that lent its name to the justification of injustice.

Prophetic Reaction: Conversion, Chastisement, Hope of Liberation

The word pronounced by Archbishop Romero was uncompromisingly severe in its denunciation of injustice and those responsible for it. Archbishop Romero's religious awareness was simply irreconcilable with atrocities that strike at the very heart of God. He was no more able to keep silent than was Jesus in similar circumstances.

First of all, he had to pronounce God's radical "no" to this world that destroys and crushes God's creatures. However, Archbishop Romero was not a simple prophet of doom, any more than were the prophets of Israel or Jesus himself. Ultimately the severity of his denunciation was in the service of the good news: even for this sin-ridden society there is hope of salvation, and liberation in history. The prophets were not content with observing and denouncing the sinfulness of their society. Their reaction was salvific. Not only their demand for conversion, but even their announcement of the wrath to come was uttered for the purpose of actualizing the possibility of salvation. However, their determination to utter concrete denunciations was of supreme importance, and this not only because they were driven to condemn what was obviously contrary to the will of God, but because they felt the crucial importance of endowing the process of authentic conversion and authentic salvation with content and orientation.

The same was true of Archbishop Romero's propheticism— his reaction to the sin of the world. His nuances, however, were different, in two ways. On the theological level, as a prophet called during the time following the definitive Christ event, Archbishop Romero placed more emphasis on hope of salvation. He was convinced, in virtue of God's victorious manifestation in Christ, that God's last word is surely salvation—that the mystery of God's grace is mightier than the mystery of iniquity upon which I have expatiated so extensively above. In this sense his prophetic charism went hand in hand with his pastoral office of confirming the hope of his people.

On the historical level, Archbishop Romero historicized the mechanisms of salvation differently. The prophets of Israel asserted that God would save God's people. Archbishop Romero proclaimed this salvation as well. But Archbishop Romero insisted that God's salvation would come through the Salvadoran people—a people imbued with a spirit of liberation in which, now explicitly, now implicitly, there was so much Christian spirit. Archbishop Romero was able to posit this relationship between salvation and the people because his time had known the phenomenon of social emancipation, something unheard-of in the time of the prophets. However, he adopted the core teaching of Second Isaiah that the suffering that comes upon one person or the people when they seek to establish justice has a salvific effect.

1. *Call to Conversion:* Week after week, Archbishop Romero denounced oppression and repression, and week after week as well, he issued his call to conversion. As their shepherd, he summoned all Salvadorans to conversion. He called for a personal renewal on the part of all. As a prophet, however, more than anything else he demanded the conversion of those re-

sponsible for the fundamental sin. For him the content, the structure, and the direction of concrete conversion were all determined by the concrete reality of the sin of society in this particular time and place. Instead of a lengthy rehearsal of all of Archbishop Romero's demands on all of those responsible for this sin, let me limit my examination to the call to conversion he addressed to the oligarchy.

The basic criterion of conversion, Archbishop Romero insisted, was the elimination of the objective and fundamental sin for which the oligarchy was responsible. A supposed interior conversion did not suffice, he forthrightly warned the oligarchy. "To the rich, too, I say that a spiritual poverty—a kind of desire, but an inefficacious desire—is not enough" (July 10, 1979).

Salvation is for the oligarchy too. "Let them come and they shall be saved" (September 2, 1979). But there was a very precise condition:

> They shall be saved only if they begin to do what Christ wills: only if they abandon a lavish life lived at the expense of the masses of the poor . . . [ibid.]. Let them cease their violent quietus of those of us who are extending this invitation, and especially let them stop murdering those of us who toil for a more just distribution of the power and wealth of our country [February 24, 1980].

Let the oligarchy abandon their injustice and violence, and salvation will be theirs. Archbishop Romero never tired of repeating this. His message was constructive, but he combined his positive pastoral concern with the forthrightness of his demands. There will be salvation for the oligarchy only when they cease to be an oligarchy and place their resources at the service of the people:

> I call on the oligarchy to cooperate in the popular process. You are the principal agents of change in this hour of destiny. On you depends, in large part, the cessation of this violence. Be reconciled with God and your fellow human beings [March 16, 1979]. I wish to issue a brotherly,

pastoral call to the oligarchy to be converted and live. Share what you are and have [February 24, 1980].

This radical conversion of the oligarchy's behavior, values, and interests would be incomplete, in Archbishop Romero's eyes, unless it were to bear lasting fruit. And so he constantly reiterated the need for structural change—for a conversion not only of the persons responsible for oppression, but also of the structures of that oppression. Archbishop Romero was only being consistent with his prophetic view of reality. Individual, personal conversion was necessary and good; but the prophetic requirement would not be met until reality as well was converted and transformed—until the reality of sin came to be, or be more like, the Reign of God:

> A genuine Christian conversion today must discover the social mechanisms that make marginalized persons of the worker or *campesino*. Why do the poor, the *campesinos,* have income only in the coffee, cotton, and sugar seasons? Why does this society have to have unemployed *campesinos,* underpaid workers, and persons who have to work for less than a just wage? We must all ferret out these mechanisms, not as sociologists or economists, but as Christians—lest we be accomplices of a machinery that afflicts our people with ever-increasing poverty, marginalization, and need. . . . Only then shall we be able to find true peace, in justice. And so the church supports whatever fosters structural change [December 16, 1979].

What Archbishop Romero demanded of the oligarchy and its economic structures, he demanded as well of the military and the military institution, of legislators and judges and the legislative and juridical structures, of journalists and the structures of the media, of clergy and the church institution. He refused to reduce conversion to a purely intentional act on the part of the subject, who, through religious mechanisms, thought it possible to stand apart from concrete, historical sin. Conversion meant an actual transformation of hearts that had become, as Paul says, total darkness, hearts that were causing the death of the masses. And it meant an effective transformation of the heart—that is, the application of this transformation to structures, that these structures might now give life to the masses of the poor.

2. *Proclamation of the Wrath to Come:* Archbishop Romero rarely spoke of God's punishment in the terminology of the prophets of Israel, or attributed punishment directly to God as an explicit action on God's part superadding vindictive suffering to the suffering that already existed. He did employ the classic prophetic rhetorical style on occasion, as when he spoke of a rampant sexual immorality: "We are astounded that God should still have patience, and not treat us still worse than he is treating us by our own fault. He might have rained down fire on this Sodom" (March 18, 1979).

For Archbishop Romero, the divine punishment in store would be the consequence of our own sinful acts. Hence we must distinguish between the pain and suffering of the people on the one hand, a suffering due to social sin, and on the other, the pain and suffering that has come and is yet to come upon the ones responsible. He did not understand the people's suffering as God's punishment: on the contrary, as we shall see below, he understood it as a salvific element for a liberation at last at hand. By contrast, he understood as intrinsic punishment the dismal prospects of those responsible for injustice.

The current national disaster, the unpopularity and successive failures of official political and economic projects, were regarded by Archbishop Romero as punishment that had at long last been visited upon the oppressors. And he prophesied that their sin would continue to fall back on the heads of its perpetrators. He repeatedly warned the rich, "Find a way to detach yourselves in good time, out of love—before these goods are violently wrenched away from you . . ." (November 11, 1979). "There is still time for you to remove your rings—before you lose your hands" (January 13, 1980). To politicians who boasted of their "reforms" he said, "Blood-soaked land will never be fertile, and bloody reforms will never bear fruit" (March 16, 1980). To authors, scholarly and popular, to the dissimulators of torture, disappearances, and death, he said, "One day all this darkness will come to light" (June 21, 1979). We must not see, in these prophecies, any desire for vengeance, or any glee to be taken in the misfortunes of others. What we have here is simply prophetic foresight: sin will return upon those who commit it. Those responsible for oppression will be victims of the contradiction they themselves have generated.

Even in speaking of the church, Archbishop Romero predicted the possibility of its sinfulness falling back on its own head. As we have observed above, Archbishop Romero was very proud of his archdiocese, and saw a hopeful present and future for a church of the poor and a church of martyrs. But this did not deprive him of his clear view of the future of the church. In his Fourth Pastoral Letter he denounced what a number of base communities had been complaining of: "the foot-dragging, antipastoral spirit with which certain priests, religious communities, and other pastoral ministers react to efforts of renewal and adaptation on the part of others who feel inspired to adopt our own pastoral approach" (no. 26). Archbishop Romero's comment was expressed in terms of the popular view: change will come, with or without the church. The challenge to the church is to be able to accompany the people in this process—to be "in on" the changes that are gradually crystallizing into the Reign of God. Otherwise the church will be "historically marginalized" (no. 26). This would be the church's punishment were it ever to be so unfortunate as to commit the sin of abandoning the people.

The most severe punishment Archbishop Romero foresaw was the possible multiplication of prevailing conflicts to the point of a wholesale blood bath. If those responsible for oppression were not converted, if they failed to make radical changes in their behavior, if they made no attempt to remedy the outrages listed in Archbishop Romero's denunciations, then, he feared, peace would be out of the question. If they refused to hear "the voices that express the anguish of the people," then they were "heading for a violent end" (September 23, 1979). If they applied no remedy to this teeming injustice, then all that remained for our country would be "solutions penned in blood" (ibid.).

These chilling warnings must not be interpreted, at least in the first instance, as an expression of Archbishop Romero's approval of "solutions written in blood." At the same time, neither must they be understood as a blanket condemnation of the same. Archbishop Romero left the door open when it came to the legitimacy of an insurrection, or even to the possibility that such might be the only solution for the problems of our land. In their first meaning, Archbishop Romero's warnings are to be understood as a prophetic proclamation of the punishment in store for those responsible for oppression. Once conflict has broken out, it will do no good to stand there and wring our hands over it. Nothing will hold it back then. It will only be the condign punishment for long years of oppressive, repressive systems. It will be the objective fruit of sin.

3. *Hope of Liberation:* As a prophet, Archbishop Romero was the consoler of his people. Amidst the misery of reality — "everything is a shambles here, a disaster; one would have to be mad to deny it" (January 7, 1979) — Archbishop Romero was yet the prophet of hope, pronouncing his word of comfort upon the people in the name of God. "How often I have wondered, here in El Salvador: What can we do? Is there no solution? At such moments, filled with hope and faith — and not only with a divine faith, but with a human one as well, for I believe in human beings — I say: 'Yes! There is a solution!' " (February 18, 1979).

Here we have a most revealing expression of Archbishop Romero's experience of nature and grace. His experience of grace was surely decisive for maintaining his hope. God wills the life of God's people. Great is the sin of the land; but the mercy of God will always be greater. Archbishop Romero compared the situation in our country to that of the Prodigal. We, too, are in tatters, destitute, and grovelling in misery. And when this crushed people returns to God it finds not resentment, but "God's arms outstretched" (March 16, 1980). And this God who can forgive, who "wills not the death of sinner, but rather that the sinner be converted and live," wills the liberation of the people as well. In the face of so many signs of hopelessness, Archbishop Romero repeated time and again: "Let us believe with the faith the prophet had when he proclaimed to the captives of Babylon a liberation that seemed never to come, and yet that eventually came, because God does not tell lies" (February 18, 1979). But along with hope in God, Archbishop Romero expressed hope in the people, both at the Christian level, where they are the sowers of seeds of liberation, and at the organizational level, which holds the promise of the shaping of a new society.

Perhaps this is the moment for a brief analysis of the relationship between the people as such, and the people organized in the hope of liberation. When Archbishop Romero defended the right of the people to organize, he surely did so in the name of a natural right of all human beings to organize. But he did so above all because an organized people represent an actual, concrete manner of overcoming structural injustice. On this account he not only defended the abstract right to organize; he positively encouraged the people to organize. In its broadest possible formulation—but a very basic one—he saw the people as El Salvador's opportunity for salvation. This is why he was so concerned both to give the people some direction, and to criticize them—and this both as a people, and precisely as organized.

Let me first analyze how he criticized the people, and let me explain why I treat his criticism here instead of above, where I examined his denunciations. The organized people are substantially the *people*—that is, they belong to the group of the oppressed, and not to the group of those responsible for basic oppression. Archbishop Romero did not divide society into three groups, the powerful on the right and the popular organizations on the left, with a hypothetical center between them. Consistent with his prophetic view of reality, he saw only two basic groups. Thus when asked about his attitude toward the "forces of the left," he replied, "I don't call them the forces of the left, I call them the forces of the people. What they call the left are the people. The 'left' is the organization of the people, and its demands are the demands of the people" (interview of March 19, 1980). Not that the organized people did not have their sins. It was just that Archbishop Romero did not see these sins as part of the basic sin of the oppressor. This is the most fundamental reason why I did not examine his criticism of the popular organizations in my treatment of his denunciations. He did denounce popular organizations. But he used a different tone, as we are about to see.

Archbishop Romero was primarily concerned to denounce any absolutization of organization:

My dear brothers and sisters of the popular political organizations: You are in danger of falling into the absolutization that I denounce in my Fourth Pastoral Letter, and
of erecting simply your own notions into the sole criterion
of your behavior [October 28, 1979]. It is a good thing for
the people to organize, and as I have said a thousand
times, the church defends the right of the people to organize. But noble as the intent may be from which it
springs, even organization can be prostituted for false worship—when it is absolutized, when it is transformed into
a supreme value [November 4, 1979].

It is important to observe that Archbishop Romero viewed
this absolutization as an evil because it meant seeking organization for its own sake and "not for the greater service of the
people" (October 28, 1979). Organization goes too far, and becomes evil, when "all other interests are subordinated to it, even
the interests of the people" (November 4, 1979).

Second, he denounced the lack of unity between the organizations and the people, as also among the various organizations themselves. His denunciation of the former failing rings
with pathos: "When I believe my organization to be absolute, I
no longer have to maintain a dialogue with anyone. I have the
solution in hand. Let them come to me. I need go to no one"
(August 12, 1979). And once more he spelled out the negative
consequences for the people. "In this hour of our country's agony, another crime is the absolutization of the popular organizations" (ibid.). And when sectarianism is an obstacle to the
establishment of dialogue and the striking of an alliance with
any other kind of popular organization, the "most serious loss
is that a potential popular force is actually transformed into an
obstacle to the people's interest, and to any deep-reaching social
change" (Fourth Pastoral Letter, no. 49).

Third, he denounced excessive politicization, not because politicization is unnecessary and not legitimate, but because when
it goes too far it "offends the sensibilities of the people" (January 13, 1980). Excessively politicized organizations "toy
with the noble sentiments of the mothers of the disappeared.
They merely manipulate these sentiments for their own objec-

tives ..." (October 28, 1979). In some cases they have gone so far as to belittle religious sentiments, and this Archbishop Romero could not abide. "I do not think that this is the way you build a land of the free. Do not destroy religious sentiments. Place them in the genuine service of an active, living people" (January 13, 1980).

Finally, Archbishop Romero denounced the excesses of violence and terrorism. He was not naive here. He admitted the legitimacy of violence in particular cases, and understood the complexity of the phenomenon of the organizations, which can go out of control, and then these organizations make mistakes. But neither did he mince words. Excessive, disproportionate violence, or acts of terrorism, do not humanize the people. His denunciation was straightforward: "Pride of organization, the pride of the head that will not bow, entails a far graver humiliation: that of going about with bloodstained hands" (September 9, 1979).

Archbishop Romero's criticism, then, when need be, was also crystal-clear, as clear as his call to conversion. But unlike his denunciations of those responsible for oppression and repression, Archbishop Romero's warnings to the popular organizations were intended as criticism of something basically good, however much it might stand in need of improvement.

> In the balance, my criticism is not a negative one. On the contrary, I recognize your great achievements (in which, for that matter, the church has helped you): your magnificent defense of the right of organization, your defense of the just demands of the people. In criticizing certain negative points I am precisely expressing my solidarity. I am only asking you: Do not lose credibility yourselves. Do not become repressive yourselves [October 28, 1979]. It is urgent that the popular organizations mature, that they may come to accomplish their mission as interpreters of the will of the people [February 24, 1980].

Archbishop Romero's criticism was forthright, then; but so was its tone and intent. He discerned great generosity in the popular organizations—a great sense of dedication to the people, and a desire to walk with them shoulder to shoulder. In a word, he saw an honorable struggle. All of this he regarded as a positive factor for the liberation of El Salvador. Furthermore, he regarded these organizations as necessary. "They are indispensable to the liberation process" (interview in *Prensa Latina,* February 15, 1980).

His esteem for the popular organizations, and his awareness of their crucial importance, were in no way diminished by his equally clear awareness that their growth, and the opposition this growth would arouse, could generate armed conflict. By no stretch of the imagination was Archbishop Romero in favor of war or insurrection. As I have said, he would have regarded it as the condign punishment of an unjust society. But he was willing to accept it as a last resort—accept it if it was inevitable, accept it if it was necessary for liberation.

> When a dictatorship gravely offends against human rights and the common good of the nation—when tyranny becomes intolerable, and channels of dialogue, understanding, and rationality are closed off—then the church speaks of the legitimate right of insurrectional violence [ibid.]. The church admits the legitimacy of insurrection when all peaceful means have been exhausted [interview in the Caracas *Diario,* March 19, 1980].

As pastor and shepherd, Archbishop Romero of course sought to preclude the necessity of this extreme solution. He sought to humanize all means of struggle. But as a prophet, he was consistent to the end: insurrection could be not only just, it could actually be the sole just solution for the problems of the poor.

Archbishop Romero's hope for popular liberation was not based merely on an accumulation of power in the people's own hands. It was based on the Christian paradox of "hope against hope" (see Rom. 4:18)—the hope of a crucified people. But, like Second Isaiah, he believed that the people's suffering is salvific, and that it will lead to liberation:

> I am sure that so much spilled blood, and so much sorrow occasioned to the families of so many victims, will not have

been in vain. . . . This blood and sorrow will water and fe-
cundate new and ever more numerous seeds — Salvadorans
who will come to an awareness of the responsibility they
have to build a society that is more just and more humane — and will fructify in the daring, urgent, and radical
structural reforms of which our country has such need
[January 27, 1980].

Archbishop Romero located the concrete, actual pathways of
liberation, as they gradually appeared, and his unshakable hope
in God, in a dialectic. Means and hope each provided a basis
for the other. And unfailingly, his last word, historical and theological, was always a word of hope: "The scream of this people
for liberation is a cry that mounts to God, and can no longer be
held in check" (January 27, 1980). "Upon these ruins the glory
of the Lord will shine!" (January 7, 1979).

Archbishop Romero's message of comfort was a message
based on the transcendent mystery of God — on the mystery of
God's love that is greater than the mystery of iniquity — and on
a people anointed by the Spirit of God. Without either polly-
annaish optimism or the pessimism of merely human calculations, Archbishop Romero believed in a new Salvadoran society,
and by conveying this hope of his own he kept up the hope of
his people.

When he had to choose a name for the historical realization
of this hope, he chose the one that most faithfully reflected
God's prophetic will for the people: "the people's project." We
have seen his criticism of this people. His hope for it was greater.
And it was a solid hope, since he could see that God's promise
was already being fulfilled: in the raised consciousness, the organization, the generosity, the solidarity of the people, the dispossessed, the poor — and simultaneously, in the grassroots
communities, in a church that was persecuted and therefore was
the vessel of the Spirit of Jesus. On grounds of the little that
had already been accomplished, Archbishop Romero believed
in magnificent things to come. Thus he maintained his hope in
the midst of difficulties, and was the consoler of the people in
the midst of their affliction. To the very end, Archbishop Romero's prophetic word was a word of hope of liberation.

The Theological Dimension of the Prophetic Word

Under examination up to this point has been the concrete, historical content of Archbishop Romero's utterances. Theoretically, this or other similar content could have been pronounced by other, not explicitly believing persons. But Archbishop Romero pronounced it as a prophet speaking in the name of God. He pronounced it with the awareness of the prophets of Israel — the awareness of someone who is "giving God a voice." Archbishop Romero made pronunciations on concrete historical affairs, yes. But he did so "in God's name," and he insisted on this point. Thus his word had an essential theological dimension, which I shall now briefly consider.

The theological dimension of Archbishop Romero's utterances appears at two levels. On a first, more basic level, the meaning of this dimension is that, through the content of his words, something of the mystery of God — and something very basic — can be revealed. From what I have already said, it should be clear that this mystery reveals itself as the mystery of a love that efficaciously wills the life of its creatures, and hence denounces a death-dealing sin and proclaims salvation from this death and this sin. But the formality of the mystery of God appears, as well. Through the concrete, historical traits of Archbishop Romero's words are revealed the formal traits of God's mystery. I have already described the concrete content of his words. My purpose has been to show all the richness of this content, in order that now, as I come to characterize the formality of his word as God's word, I may not be tempted — an all too frequent temptation — to banalize the word of God.

On a second, more strictly ecclesiological level, the prophetic word as word of God both requires of the church that it continue to hear this same word, and bestows upon it the actual ability to do so, by introducing into the church a tension between being a "hearer of the word" and yet the "depository of faith." This is not only of prime importance theologically, but is of the greatest currency, as well, in El Salvador today, since what would seem to be uppermost in the minds of the highest-ranking members of the hierarchy is a determination to dissolve this tension by doing away with prophecy, rather than a determination to continue in the humble discipleship of the word of God today, as Archbishop Romero practiced that discipleship.

The Prophetic Word as Word of God

The prophetic word, as the word of God, has certain characteristics. Far from being casual or contingent, these characteristics correspond to the very reality of God. Archbishop Romero did not explicitate this correspondence reflexively; but he did so in act. Through the very awareness with which he pronounced his word, he actualized, rendered present, the basic characteristics of the boundless mystery of God.

1. The prophetic word is an *ultimate* word. It expresses the very truth of God. Accordingly, it wins its specific efficaciousness not from analysis, reflection, or argumentation—important and necessary as these are in view of other considerations—but rather from the fact of its enunciation directly in the name of the truth of God. "God does not tell lies" (February 18, 1979); "it is the living God who speaks" (June 10, 1979), Archbishop Romero would often say. This word is self-authenticating, simply in virtue of being the truth—simply because it is "clear and transparent as a mountain stream."[7]

God's word is ultimate, impossible to manipulate, and peremptory for those who genuinely love the truth—for those who are willing to seek the truth and accept it when it comes to light. This is how Archbishop Romero, such a passionate lover of the truth, understood the word of God. In one of his homilies he recounted an especially meaningful anecdote about something that had happened on his trip back from Puebla. As he had turned to walk away with his luggage after passing customs inspection, he heard someone say: "There goes the truth." And he added in his homily, simply, profoundly: "Yes, there is nothing being smuggled in my suitcase. No lies. I carry only the truth" (February 18, 1979).

Elementary as it may seem, we must remember that the prophetic word is ultimate because it is truth, and hence a mediation of God. Through that word God is truth *in actu.* To utter the word of prophecy, and feel the weight of its urgency, is to accept at one and the same time the ultimacy of God and the ultimacy of truth. Conversely, the historical prophetic word is God's way of continuing to be truthful. The historical word of prophecy is God's historical self-manifestation as truth.

2. The prophetic word is a *sovereign* word. Nowhere in creation need the prophet not cry that word. No created reality, not even a reality that may be a mediation of the will of God, is exempt from the criticism and enlightenment of the word of prophecy.

That this was Archbishop Romero's understanding is evinced in his remarks concerning the false prophet Amaziah, who seemed to be arguing so reasonably against Amos: "Off with you, visionary, flee to the land of Judah! There earn your bread by prophesying, but never again prophesy in Bethel; for it is the king's sanctuary and a royal temple" (Amos 7:12–13). Archbishop Romero's comment on the passage: "In that temple you must prophesy as the king wishes!" (July 15, 1979). The temple, the king, even the shrine at Bethel were regarded as mediations of the will of God. Really now, what purpose could it serve to utter a prophetic word, a new word of God, precisely in the house of God—and furthermore against Israel, the chosen people?

To this attempt to domesticate, and thereby adulterate, the word of God, Archbishop Romero responded by insisting on the absolute sovereignty of that word. Nothing created, whether in the religious sphere or in the civil, can stipulate limits to this word. God cannot be "cut down to size." God is greater than all things, and must be allowed to be God. No aspect of existence or history may be sacralized, absolutized, "as if God were not sovereign over all the world and could not send his messengers wherever he might wish to send them" (July 15, 1979). Hence Archbishop Romero's frequent use of Peter's celebrated dictum: "It is better to obey God than men" (e.g., July 15, 1979).

The prophetic word is one of the forms of God's own self-manifestation in history—one of the ways in which God over-flows the limits in which historical institutions could wish to enclose the divine transcendence and thereby (albeit invoking the very name of God) diminish it, "cut it down to size."

3. The prophetic word is a *historical* word. It bears on the

concrete historical. It must refer to secular history, and not be confined, not be reduced to the orbit of worship and religion. This was abundantly clear from Archbishop Romero's own preaching. But he also expounded it as a *de jure* reality. "God does not despise concrete deeds" (February 18, 1979). "Any preaching that felt no need to enflesh God's salvific project in the tragic, painful, or hopeful vicissitudes of our reality, would not be authentic Christian preaching" (December 24, 1978).

The prophetic word uncovers the will of God in history. It is not proclaimed on the basis of what is *already* known of God and the will of God, a priori and antecedently to concrete history. It is proclaimed on the basis of God's *ongoing manifestation* in history. "Here are God's pathways—the pathways of our family, private, and national life" (December 7, 1978). And the prophetic word is uttered amidst and upon that which at any given moment constitutes the most fundamental datum of history—wherever there is no room for casuistry and still less for compromise, wherever the will of God is clear as noonday. It is for this reason, and not out of a spirit of masochism—least of all in virtue of a desire, hypocritically imputed to him by some, to slander our country—that Archbishop Romero consistently pronounced his word upon the tragic history of this land. We must extend God's history "into the concrete facts of our kidnapped citizens, our tortured citizens—into our own sorrowful history," he declared. "For it is there that we must find our God" (December 24, 1978). The word of prophecy, then, is God's way of achieving incarnation in concrete history, and of decreeing, from within that incarnation—and not on the basis of some abstract principle or other—the divine will for history.

4. The prophetic word is a *partisan* word. If anything is clear in authentic prophecy, beginning with the cries of the prophets of Israel and continuing to Mary's Magnificat and the words of Jesus, it is that God tears down the mighty from their thrones and exalts the lowly (Luke 1:52). Paradoxically, the word of the God who is the creator of all things and sovereign over the whole of history, shows partiality. It does so because this is what God has decreed, and for the reason shown above: the prophetic word bears on the basics of history, and to the divine eyes there is nothing more basic—nothing more basically abominable—

than to have to behold a creation vitiated by the oppression some human beings inflict on others. To show partiality, then, to take sides, is not being arbitrary; it is simply being faithful to God, faithful to the work of the divine hands.

And this is how Archbishop Romero understood prophetic partiality. His word was not partisan in any narrow, petty sense of the word. But it was clearly partial to the oppressed. Why? Because, as he was accustomed to say, the poor touch the very heart of God. "To be concerned with the interests of God's little ones—this is transcendence" (September 30, 1979). Thereby he located the poor within the very reality of God. And he justified his partisanship by the very reality of God. This he did *in actu,* abundantly, in his homilies. In his Louvain address he reflected on it more systematically:

> We believe in a Jesus who came to bring life in fullness, and we believe in a living God who gives life to human beings and wills that they actually live. These radical truths of faith really become truths, and radical truths, when the church genuinely enters into the life and death of its people. Then the church will be faced with the same option as confronts every human being: to favor life or to favor death. Surely it is clear that there can be no neutral ground here. Either we serve the life of Salvadorans, or we are the accomplices of their death. And here we have the historical mediation of the very heart of our faith: either we believe in a God of life, or we serve the idols of death.

And so Archbishop Romero took sides with God, which is shown most clearly of all in the word of prophecy. Through this word God actually divides oppressors from oppressed—divides "you" from "my people." And thus we have an expression of God's primordial option for the little—not an arbitrary option, to be sure, but a loving one, an option for those whose very lives are threatened or actually extinguished. The word of prophecy insists that the universality of the mystery of God passes by way of this partiality.

5. The prophetic word is a *novel* word. Why? Because it is historical. Whether the prophets of Israel practiced their proph-

ecy at the apogee of the monarchy or in its decline, on their
native soil or in exile, are matters of consequence for the prophetic word. Prophecy without the novel word would be a *contrad-
ictio in terminis.* Theologically it would imply a formal denial of
the inexhaustible nature of God. Thus the prophet proclaims
new words, changing words, to the scandal both of those who
believe themselves already to be in possession of all truth—those
who think that they can stake out the limits of history and its
interpretation—and of those who (with more sophistication, and
seemingly altogether piously) regard themselves as authorized
to invalidate any attempt at novelty by invoking the eternal transcendence of the mystery of God.

As if responding to this objection—the most radical objection
of all, from the standpoint of faith—Archbishop Romero said
something by which he could scarcely help scandalizing the ears
of the pious: "The transcendent is not enough. How nice, to be
able to write about the transcendent!" (September 9, 1979).

No one can question Archbishop Romero's earnestness in
citing the transcendence of God with such insistence. But neither can we question the fact that he did so not as if he grasped
or possessed that transcendence somehow; rather he simply rendered that transcendence present in the vagaries of history. This
is why he uttered a novel word wherever the history of God
became novel and demanded it. And so, more doctrinally in his
pastoral letters, more prophetically in his homilies, he unfailingly addressed the new realities with which he was faced in the
sociopolitical situation, in the persecution of the church, or in
new styles of ecclesial life like the base communities.

I could not possibly present all of Archbishop Romero's "new
words" here. But let us recall at least some of his symbolic
deeds—which are also vehicles of the prophet's message—
which, precisely by virtue of their radical novelty, attracted so
much attention. Once and only once in the history of El Salvador, all of the churches of the archdiocese except the cathedral
were closed on Sunday—so that all the faithful who wished
could gather to celebrate one and the same Mass. Once and
only once in the recent history of Salvador, the Archbishop of
San Salvador did not attend the solemn investiture of a President of the Republic. Once and only once in the recent history

of El Salvador, the Archbishop of San Salvador declined to make the Cathedral of the Divine Savior available to the nuncios and the government to celebrate Pope's Day—although he celebrated it (and in the cathedral) with his people.

Precisely because their novelty was grasped by the people, these novel deeds of Archbishop Romero constituted a mediation of the intrinsic novelty of the mystery of God. They lent embodiment to another beautiful expression of Irenaeus, "the Spirit's slow familiarization with history." God's transcendence does not mean that God is equidistant from all historical events. It means that the mystery of God's love, truth, mercy, justice, and so on, is expressed differently in different circumstances. Hence the importance of the new prophetic word: God's transcendence must be shown to be present in its incarnations in history.

6. The prophetic word is a *conflictive* word. After all, it is partisan, and it is novel. And it is a powerful expression of the will of God in contradiction of the sin of the world. It is not, then—at least not precisely as prophetic word—a conciliatory word, a negotiating word, or a word that stoops compassionately to human frailty. God pronounces words of mercy and consolation through the prophets, yes—but only after denunciation and condemnation.

The word of prophecy is conflictive because it is uttered on the radical, absolute levels of "yes" and "no," where there are no intermediate gradations. Archbishop Romero was altogether conscious of the conflicts produced by his word. But he correctly attributed them to the objectivity of that word, not to any conflictive subjectivity on the part of the prophet who uttered it. "If it is the genuine word of God, it contains explosive material, and few are willing to carry it on their person. If it were defused, no one would be afraid of it" (September 9, 1979).

Thus we also grasp the demanding, incorruptible nature of the mystery of God. Conflict? To be sure. But none other than God initiated this conflict—God whose word is "sharper than any two-edged sword" (Heb. 4:12–13), scrutinizing what is concealed and exposing what is false. It is God who is explosive—provided we have the courage to let God be God, and attempt no manipulation of what is divine. And the word of prophecy manifests this, as well.

7. The prophetic word is a *fragile, defenseless, contradicted* word. The source of its strength is likewise the source of its weakness. It is uttered in the name of God, but can offer no other evidence of this than the sheer fact of its utterance. The world rejects this word in a number of ways, some of them crude, others more subtle. Archbishop Romero was attacked crudely, as we know. But he was also attacked subtly, by way of disparagement, and through the invocation of other "prophets."

Jesus was disparaged by his fellow Galileans as the son of a carpenter. Just so, Archbishop Romero was disparaged with allegations that his words were not his own—that he was being used—that is, ultimately, that his word was not the word of God. With keen psychological insight, Archbishop Romero himself analyzed this mechanism of calumniation and its purpose: to exempt the hearer from the obligation to accept the word.

> This is the terrible thing about our society—a society in which persons reject the word of the gospel when it does not agree with their selfishness, when it does not suit their injustice. Then a mountain of questions arise: "Where did he get all these ideas? Who is his manager? These can't be his own ideas." And all the other accusations you can invent when you have already rejected someone or something [July 8, 1979].

And in the train of the calumny campaign marched all the false prophets, civil and ecclesiastical. They, too, invoked God, and attacked Archbishop Romero in the name of God. But at bottom they were only echoing the false prophet Amaziah: Prophesy as the king directs! Archbishop Romero was consummately aware of this. "We have more than enough sycophants, more than enough false prophets, and more than enough—in times of conflict like ours—pens for hire and words for sale" (February 18, 1979). There were more than enough of "those who vie with one another in perpetrating injustice and oppression, in living as lavishly and ostentatiously as possible, and in worship that does no honor to God" (July 15, 1979).

The attacks, persecution, and slander the prophet must suffer are the historical expression of the most profound of all Christian propositions upon the mystery of God: that of the divine abasement or *kenōsis*. God stands before the world in truth, love, and justice—but in helplessness, as well. Men and women make sport of, reject, and persecute God, to the point of the total abasement of the divinity in the cross of Jesus. The frailty of the prophetic word shows forth the divine weakness, the product of God's ultimate solidarity with the poor.

The Prophetic Word and the Faith of the Church

Archbishop Romero prophesied from within the church. In fact, he understood his prophecy as nothing more than his individual, personal expression of the propheticism of his archdiocese as a whole.

> I have never felt I was a prophet in the sense of being the only prophet of the people. I know that you and I, the people of God, together, compose the prophetic people. I am happy to say that, thank God, there is a prophetic awakening in our archdiocese: in the base church community, in prayer and study groups, and in this critical awareness that is developing in our Christianity, which will be a Christianity of the herd no longer; now it means to be a Christianity of awareness [July 8, 1979].

A whole archdiocese, however, will scarcely be likely to perform this prophetical activity explicitly. As we know, propheticism and the institution coexist in history in a state of tension. Prophecy comports novelty and conflict—precisely what the institution, in virtue of its very structure, is concerned to avoid. Hence the surprise and gratitude of so many Latin Americans when Archbishop Romero and several of the other bishops of our continent managed to synthesize the institutional and prophetic functions in their own persons. What I should like to examine here is the theological root of that tension, the understandable temptation of the institution to silence prophecy, and despite all, the benefit of prophecy for the church. Sadly, these

questions are anything but purely theoretical: since Archbishop
Romero's murder, the highest level of the hierarchy has been
systematically silencing his prophetic word.

1. Prophets, as such, do not speak in their own name. They
do not even speak in the name of the synagogue, the temple, or
the church. They speak directly in the name of God. They have
been chosen and sent by God, and are ultimately responsible to
God alone. As our bishop, of course, Archbishop Romero frequently invoked his formal, institutional, ecclesial authority, arguing in the name of truth and the teaching of the church. But
his propheticism had deeper roots. Propheticism is ultimately
rooted in God. "Our only greatness is openness to God, and a
readiness to answer him, with the prophets, 'Here I am Lord—
send me' " (July 8, 1979).

As one sent by God, the prophet utters a concrete, direct
word of God. A prophet is not, then, a simple preacher setting
forth a word concerning God, or a theologian reflecting on the
word of God. A prophet is, we might say, a theologian *in actu*—
someone who brings it about that God (*Theos*) pronounces a
word (*logos*) at a particular moment, a word that is particularly
appropriate for that moment. Hence the introduction of the
classic prophets' discourses by formulae ascribing them directly
to God: "Thus says the Lord, . . ." "Oracle of Yahweh, . . ." "Say
to my people, . . ." and so on. Hence also Archbishop Romero's
expressions, at crucial moments, like, "In the name of God, . . . I
beg you, I entreat you, I order you . . ." (March 23, 1980). This
was not a mere rhetorical device. It was the expression of Archbishop Romero's mission as a prophet: to speak directly in the
name of God.

As the prophet is sent by God alone, to God alone is the
prophet directly responsible. Hence propheticism's irresistible
thrust to utterance. The word must be uttered, and no argument,
not even a churchly one, can stifle it. This is how Archbishop
Romero understood his own prophetic calling, as we may readily
gather from his reflection on the call of the prophet Ezekiel.
His words seem harsh:

> The prophet's success does not consist in converting the
> people. If this occurs, then blessed be the holy name of

God. Then God will have attained the *divine* end intended through this human instrument. But if the prophet does not succeed in converting this stiff-necked people, no matter. The prophet's success lies in this—that this stiff-necked, sinful, faithless people at least recognize that it has had a prophet in its midst, who spoke to it in the name of God. The prophet's mission is a terrible one. The prophet must speak out even knowing that no one will listen. If the people pay no heed, they are lost through their own fault. The prophet has done his duty: there has been someone to tell the people, "Thus saith the Lord" [July 8, 1979].

This passage would be incomprehensible in a purely pastoral or theological perspective. God's will is not only to speak, but to be heard, to be obeyed, to cause the Reign of God to come. But the severity of Archbishop Romero's words has the advantage of showing that the word of prophecy not only is the word of God, but is the prophet's responsibility to God. Indeed, this was Archbishop Romero's conscious intent. "We are a prophetic church, dear brothers," he continued. "We cannot fall silent in a world so corrupt, so unjust. That would only be to make a terrible metaphor come true: 'Mute watchdogs: What good is a watchdog that does not bark when the treasury is threatened?' " (July 8, 1979).

2. This direct reference to God has the effect that, though it be performed within the church, the prophet's activity is raised above the level of the church and even is exercised upon the church. That is, the prophet recalls and actualizes something which, while evident objectively and in itself, is nevertheless difficult to accept: that the church is not the ultimate reality. God is greater than the church. God judges the church, and proclaims the divine will not only through established institutions, but through other channels as well.

God's "ever more"—the divine transcendence—surely appears at the ethical level. No one today denies in principle that the church is sinful; the church itself admits this fact. But the prophet says so concretely, not merely in principle, and appeals to God's authority in saying so. In other cases, the church can and should be the judge where sin is alleged. But in the case of the prophetic word, the church, like any other historical reality, is the defendant, and stands before the one, ultimate Judge. This was Archbishop Romero's own view:

> The prophet denounces the sins committed within the church, too. Why? If we bishops, popes, priests, apostolic nuncios, nuns, Catholic schools, and so on, are human beings or shaped by human beings, and we human beings are sinners, then we need someone to be *our* prophet, too, and call *us* to conversion.
>
> When criticism becomes propheticism—then the prophet tells the church, too, "Thus saith the Lord," and reads it the gospel. After all, the bishop or the priest may not be acting in conformity with the gospel. Then it is the church that must be willing to be converted, with the love with which we must all love and follow our Lord Jesus Christ [July 8, 1979].

Archbishop Romero is expressing more in these texts than a routine proposition on the sinfulness of the church. He is saying that this sinfulness can extend to all levels of the church. And he is saying, especially, that those in the church whose office it is to pass judgment on sin—the pope, the bishops, the nuncios, the priests, and so on—are by no means exempt from prophetic denunciation. After all, the latter issues from God, and not from any source inferior to these exalted ecclesiastical personages. The church and its hierarchy must *establish* criteria for a historical determination of what constitutes sin. But the prophet can enunciate criteria of sin that are unavailable to the church, criteria in terms of which the church itself is vulnerable to denunciation. When it hears, "Thus saith the Lord," the church must simply hear and be converted.

3. If the ethical word of prophecy may question the church on the basis of the fact that the church admits its sinfulness in principle, still more may it do so on the basis of the prophetic claim to speak the very truth of God, to be the ultimate way of knowing the divine will. But here a difficulty arises. If there *already exist* dogmas, social teaching, canon law, and theologies

that in given eras have held themselves out as official theologies — and especially, if there is already a deposit of revelation — then what need can the church have of individuals and communities to prophesy to it, to proclaim to it the will of God? Can it be that the church does not yet sufficiently know about God and the will of God?

These questions are not rhetorical. If the church has jealously defended anything, it has jealously defended its function as the depository of God's truth. And this is as it should be. But the church may do this in a correct way: by admitting, in the name of God's truth, whose depository it is, the possibility of a current word of prophecy coming from God; or it may do it in an incorrect way: by effectively precluding this possibility. History is the everlasting witness of the concrete tension between the current truth of God in prophecy and that truth as already possessed and jealously guarded.

If I may be permitted a brief historical excursus, with a view to shedding light on the present: let us recall the fact that classic propheticism vanished in Israel precisely at the moment when, around the fifth century B.C., the Pentateuch — the first five books of the Old Testament, called the Torah, the law — was approaching the zenith of its influence on Jewish religion. By now these books had come to be regarded as an inspired canon. That is, they manifested to the people the will of God as already known. A doctrinal corpus had appeared. Official persons called scribes had appeared on the scene to interpret this corpus. In principle, therefore, why should it continue to be necessary to have recourse to prophecy in order to know the will of God? Thus prophetic inspiration now gave way to the inspiration of the scribes. At the theological level, what was occurring, basically, was that *another* channel had been found, distinct from the prophetic, for learning the will of God.

We need not dwell at length on parallels between the situation of Jewish religion in the last centuries B.C. and that of the church today. It is remarkable, however, that, just as with the people of Israel in those days, the Latin American peoples today grasp the need for a prophetic word, feel it to be missing when it does not exist, and are grateful for it whenever it appears on the scene, though it be critical of themselves. They have an intuitive grasp of the immediacy of a direct word from God. Compare Israel's constant recollection of its prophets—an Elijah, a Jeremiah. In the last centuries before Christ the people of God still looked forward to the appearance of a prophet; hence the popular stir at the appearance of John the Baptist or Jesus. And yet the people had the law. In the same fashion, it is remarkable how much commotion Archbishop Romero and other prophets have occasioned in Latin America. There are a number of reasons for it, surely; but the theological dimension can scarcely be ignored. God's people, at least unconsciously, ever await the arrival of God's word—await a prophet who will tell them in the name of God things that reach beyond whatever they may know "institutionally." They do not fear this word, though it comes to judge themselves. They are eager to hear it. Intuitively they know that the prophetic word of God must necessarily be helpful, which is not always the case with words of God pronounced in the church.

Theologically, the prophetic word introduces a powerful tension into the church. Today's church admits this in principle. But in practice there are serious problems. In the first place, the church possesses a doctrinal word *about* God, a word *concerning* God, while the prophet utters a word *of* God, *from* God. To be sure, Archbishop Romero, like the prophets of Israel, appealed to the highest doctrinal sources. But these sources preserve, directly, only a doctrinal word *about* God, an orthodox word. *In directo,* the prophetic word is a word *of* God, *from* God: "Thus saith the Lord. . . ." In principle, this means assigning priority to the word of God over words about God—to God's revelation over its theological or even dogmatic elaboration. Vatican Council II proclaimed this, in its own fashion, when it asserted: "This magisterium is not above the word of God, but at its service" (*Dei Verbum*, no. 10). Today's prophets implement this principle by actually observing that priority.

In the second place, while the church claims to possess the word of God contained in revelation, prophets claim that, in addition to the divine self-manifestation in a past revelation, God works an ongoing self-manifestation in the present (with all due respect to any technical distinctions between a past, closed revelation, and God's manifestation in the present).

Prophets utter concrete, current words—speak the will of God *in actu.* Prophets do not simply repeat the words God uttered in ages past, however true those words may be; they pronounce God's current word. Of course, the prophets—and Archbishop Romero—made use of the words God had uttered in bygone times. But there was also something in the prophetic activity of the prophets that could not be deduced from anything, not even from previous revelation.

The church today has recognized the need for the prophetical dimension. The church speaks of the "signs of the times" (Matt. 16:3) as an indispensable means for recognizing the will of God. What the prophet does—something not so easy for the institutional church to do—is to list these signs concretely. The church may declare some of them important ones, and with all forthrightness, as with the condemnation of the national security regimes, or political absolutisms. But the church does not proceed beyond these still rather general determinations. The prophet, on the other hand, comes right out and says *just what it is* that these regimes do that is wrong and sinful. The prophet states the *concrete, specific* injustices of those political absolutisms *actually at hand.* Archbishop Romero astounded one and all by identifying as one of the signs of the times the sudden growth in the popular organizations, and stated that there was more hope in a popular project than elsewhere. And he said all this in the name of God, not merely because it might be appropriate to do so, or in function of certain political calculations.

4. The church must of course have a teaching *about* God, and must safeguard the *deposit* of revelation. It is the institutional church that must see to these matters. But the church must not believe that its most original and basic relationship with God is to be found at these levels. Its original, basic relationship with God occurs in prophecy, in God's *own* word, and God's *current* word. In uttering and hearing this word, the church becomes the ongoing vehicle of God's truth. And in putting it in practice it becomes the holy church. Neither dimension excludes the other, then. In the concrete, it is natural that they should be in tension. But the church must not forget where the primacy lies. This was Archbishop Romero's intuition.

We need someone to serve as our prophet, too, today, someone to call us to conversion, lest we become too comfortable with our religion, as if it were untouchable. Religion needs prophets, and thank God we have them. It would be a sad church indeed that would regard itself as sovereign over truth to the extent of rejecting all other claims to that truth [July 8, 1979].

The prophet sees to it that religion not be regarded as untouchable. Nor is this prophetic vigilance limited to the area of morals. The prophet also takes care that the church not regard itself as sovereign over the truths of faith. At this level, prophecy goes to the root of the theological question. By its very existence, the word of prophecy asks the church the tremendous question of whether it takes God seriously, or whether, by virtue of its institutional element—legitimate and necessary though this element may be in other respects—it has found a way to keep itself safe from the living word of God.

Archbishop Romero's prophetic word had a profound theological dimension. He spoke *in* the church, but as a prophet he spoke *in the name of* God. Through the concrete content of his prophetic word, and by uttering that word in a prophetical manner, he posed two basic theological questions. In *what* God does the church believe? *Does* the church believe in God? Archbishop Romero's own answer was clear. It believes in God. After all, it allows God to continue uttering the divine word—it lets God be God. Thereby it professes its faith in a God greater than all else—greater even than itself. And it believes in a God of history, a God who denounces the sin that deals death, a God who maintains the hope of the poor. It is to Archbishop Romero's great credit to have posed these two questions, which are ultimate for the church; in replying to these questions the church will vitiate or realize its essence.

Eschatological Dimension of the Prophetic Word

Things did not go well with the prophets of Israel. They were slandered, insulted, threatened, exiled, persecuted, and sometimes murdered. By Jesus' time it had become proverbial that prophets came to a bad end. John the Baptist was murdered. Jesus had to say: "O Jerusalem, Jerusalem, killing the prophets and stoning those who are sent to you!" (Matt. 23:37). The first Christians, disconcerted by the sentencing and execution of Jesus, their Messiah, found a historical logic for the catastrophe in the reflection that, after all, Jesus was a prophet (Luke 24:19,27). That said it all.

And yet these persons who ended so badly were vessels of the word of God. It is not a rhetorical question, then, to ask: Where is this word now? Where can we find it? What does death have to say about this word?

Archbishop Romero, too, came to a bad end: he was murdered. But he had reflected in advance on the relationship between the prophetic word and martyrdom, and on the survival of that word. He could do so because he exercised his prophetic activity not in isolation, but in a prophetical archdiocese that had already seen numerous martyrdoms. Let me conclude my present consideration, then, by asking why Archbishop Romero was put to death, and where his word still lives.

1. Archbishop Romero understood his approaching prophetic fate in terms of the fate of his archdiocese as a whole. He recognized that the latter was invested with great ecclesial puissance, and that this fact was promptly rendered an occasion of conflict and persecution. "If our archdiocese has been suddenly plunged in conflict, have no doubt of it, it is owing to its fidelity to the new evangelization" (March 11, 1979). And conflict invariably brought persecution in its wake. The fact was evident to Archbishop Romero—although other hierarchs were not of the same opinion—and therefore rather than wondering whether this was persecution, he wondered why the persecution. And his answer was clear. "The church is persecuted because it preaches justice" (December 9, 1979)—"because it refuses to be indifferent to, or in complicity with, the situation of sin and structural violence prevailing in our land" (June 24, 1979). The church was persecuted "because it is an annoyance" (September 23, 1979).

Archbishop Romero saw that the specific reason the church was persecuted was that it preached the word of truth. The basic danger represented by the church to the powerful was not any political power it might come to possess, but the power of truth. Hence, without the slightest hint of rhetoric, but in full knowledge that the essence of the church was at stake, he repeatedly asserted of the church: "It must be prepared not to betray the truth. If it must lose privileges, it will lose privileges, but it will always tell the truth. If it is calumniated, it knows that it is being calumniated for telling the truth" (April 22, 1979).

Thus he saw that the church was persecuted for formally the same reasons as those for which Jesus was persecuted. Jesus was persecuted for being a prophet, not directly for being political, although false accusations of political subversion were also raised against him. It was very important to Archbishop Romero to grasp the reason for Jesus' persecution, in order to understand what was really, intrinsically happening to the church, that he might have an answer for those who justified the persecution of the church, and be able to expose those who asserted that the church was being persecuted not as a religious institution but as a politicized social force. Archbishop Romero clearly saw that it was Jesus' prophetic word that occasioned his persecution. "Christ is a stumbling block, a rock of scandal. Christ is a sign of contradiction. History is repeating itself" (December 31, 1978). The church was being called what Christ had been called: "an agitator, a popular alarmist" (September 16, 1979). In the first place, then, Archbishop Romero saw that the church was persecuted not because its essence had been corrupted and not because it was seeking political power, but because it was following Christ. The church was being persecuted precisely because it was realizing its Christian essence.

In the second place, Archbishop Romero saw in the persecution of the church the verification in act of its incarnation among a people of the poor. The church was a church of the poor, and had articulated the word that the people implicitly spoke in the sheer fact of being an oppressed, crucified people. "I rejoice, brothers and sisters, that our church is persecuted precisely for its preferential option for the poor, and for seeking incarnation in the interests of the poor" (July 15, 1979). And he expressed the converse even more graphically: "How sad it would be, in a country where such horrible murders are being committed, if there were no priests among the victims! A mur-

dered priest is a testimonial to a church incarnate in the problems of the people" (June 24, 1979).

That the church was being the "voice of the voiceless"—the
modern translation of "prophetic"—Archbishop Romero saw in
the common fate of the church and the poor. This was the clearest criterion, for him, of the church's incarnation among the
people and its following of Jesus. "The church suffers the lot of
the poor—persecution. It is the glory of our church to have
mixed its blood—the blood of its priests, catechists, and communities—with the massacres of the people, and ever to have
borne the mark of persecution" (February 17, 1980).

The common lot of the poor and Jesus led Archbishop Romero to make the most radical statement on the meaning of the
persecution of the church that could be made. Far from seeing,
in its persecution, the consequence of a vitiation of the church,
he saw the mark of the true church. "Persecution is a characteristic note of the authenticity of the church. A church that
suffers no persecution, but rather enjoys the privileges and support of this world, has good reason to fear. It is not the true
church of Jesus Christ" (March 11, 1979).

It is as a member of that church, a church persecuted and
martyred for its propheticism, that Archbishop Romero antici-
pated his own fate. Although he did not customarily speak on
a personal note in his homilies, he would, from time to time,
especially during the last months of his life, make some reference to his approaching end, comparing it with the fate of Jesus
and regarding it in terms of his ultimate solidarity with his people.

> They do me an immense honor when they reject me be-
> cause I resemble, be it ever so little, Jesus Christ, who was
> also a stumbling block [December 31, 1978]. My sole com-
> fort is that Christ, too, who sought to communicate this
> great truth, was misunderstood, was called a rebel, and
> was condemned to death, as I have received death threats
> these past days [June 3, 1979].

Archbishop Romero regarded his own persecution in the
same terms as he regarded that of his archdiocese. He under-

stood that he was persecuted and threatened with death because he defended the people and maintained solidarity with them, which meant he must share their last end. But he not only accepted his fate passively, he spelled it out in so many words. When General Romero's government offered him a bodyguard, he refused, lest he detract from the sense of his propheticism:

> I hereby inform the president that, rather than my own security, what I should like to have is security and tranquility for 108 families and their "disappeared" . . . the security of all who suffer. My personal well-being, the security of my own person, is of no interest to me when I see an economic, social, and political system operating among my people that only exacerbates social differences [June 3, 1979].

Archbishop Romero's refusal to take any interest in his own security was a prophetic gesture, whereby he proclaimed that his word came from the people and was uttered in defense of the people. Thus he consistently maintained his prophetic vision of reality to the end: a vision of a humanity divided into oppressors and oppressed. If Archbishop Romero opposed the oppressors, it would have to be because he placed himself among the oppressed. And lest any doubt of this remain, he adopted the earmark of the oppressed par excellence: their insecurity. "I should like to repeat to you something I have said before: a shepherd seeks no security as long as the flock is threatened" (July 22, 1979).

With this prophetic deed Archbishop Romero maintained to the death his vision of the alternatives he had faced in life: the oppressors or the oppressed, the gods of death or the God of Jesus. Archbishop Romero was not murdered because he failed to take security measures, or because he rejected a government security team. He was murdered for a positive reason. He had made his option for the God of Jesus, and this option meant his incarnation among a people who suffer death.

2. It remains to ask what becomes of the prophet's word when the prophet has died. In Israel, prophets were persecuted in life and glorified in death. Jesus denounced this hypocrisy. "Woe to

you, you who build the prophets' tombs, when it was your own fathers who murdered them!" (Luke 11:47). "Woe to you scribes and Pharisees, you frauds! You erect tombs for the prophets and adorn the monuments of the saints" (Matt. 23:29).

There have been various reactions to Archbishop Romero's martyrdom. Some who criticized him in life have praised him after his death. But they have praised him only as a "good man," a "defender of the peace," and so on, not as a radical prophet. Others have attempted to silence his word—have tried to see to it that it would gradually die out. Those currently in power, for example, whose discourse is always so chock-full of God and religion, have never once recalled his prophetic word, a word so illuminating for the historical situation of our country. Nor did the Joint Pastoral Letter of the Salvadoran Bishops Conference (September 15, 1980) mention or cite Archbishop Romero a solitary time. Neither does that letter, either in its content or in its spirit, respond or correspond to his prophetic word—and this while pretending to define the nature of prophetic denunciation (see p. 17)! Some observers have actually seen in the Joint Pastoral a veiled attack on Archbishop Romero's propheticism. In sum, the mighty, of whatever institution, have sought to domesticate Archbishop Romero's propheticism, with either empty praise, or a step-by-step muzzling. It is not in the corridors of power, then, that Archbishop Romero's word continues to live.

And yet his word still lives. While he was still alive, and still sowing the fields of the world for a mighty harvest of the prophetic word, he himself reflected on the question of the survival of his word after his death. First of all, he regarded martyrdom as the ultimate, most powerful word of prophecy: "The voice of blood is the most eloquent of words. This archiepiscopal see, then, enjoys a special sense of security, in virtue of the testimony of blood that, in this cathedral, has become almost an ordinary voice" (June 21, 1979). This voice is the most eloquent of all because it appears on the scene as "a demand for God's justice in the face of the sin of the world," and as "the hope of those who die for an ideal" (ibid.). This is the prophet's last word, and the ultimate word of prophecy. Here denunciation and hope attain their definitive synthesis.

As the most eloquent of words, the voice of blood lives on—

but not among the powerful, of whatever cast or hue. It abides among only those who have accepted it during the prophet's lifetime. It is important to emphasize where Archbishop Romero believed that his word would survive. He did not doubt that it would survive. And he specified just where it would survive. It would not be among the mighty—not even, strictly speaking, within the church in its quality as institutional. Rather, he believed, it would survive among the true followers of Jesus as such, and among his, Oscar Romero's, people. Ever since his martyrdom, history has abundantly demonstrated that he was right: "The word remains. And this is the preacher's great comfort. My voice will pass away, but my word, which is Christ, will remain in the hearts of those who have been open to receive it" (February 17, 1978).

In an interview he granted shortly before his death, he declared, with such simplicity, but with such prophetic vision, as well, who would be the authentic heirs of his word. "If they kill me, I shall rise again in the Salvadoran people. I am not boasting; I say it with the greatest humility" (March 1980).

Finally, he believed that his prophetic word would continue to live, and be salvific, in the form of a people's hope of liberation. Precisely when it is smothered in blood, the prophetic word has a special efficacy, as Second Isaiah saw. This was Archbishop Romero's hope.

> If they manage to carry out their threats, I shall be offering my blood for the redemption and resurrection of El Salvador.... May my blood be the seed of liberty, and a sign of the hope that will soon become a reality.... May my death, if it is accepted by God, be for the liberation of my people, and as a witness of hope in what is to come [ibid.].

This was Archbishop Romero's heartfelt conviction, as a Christian, and as a human being engaged in the particular historical reality of our time and place. The word of prophecy is fragile, and so it is persecuted and annihilated. But it is also mighty—indeed, invincible. After all, it rests on the truth and justice of God. It is a word that lives on, lives on among the people, lives on amidst their best efforts for liberation. "Let the record show: from this moment forward, no one will ever slay the voice of justice . . ." (February 24, 1980).

3. In the current circumstances of our country and the church, we can do nothing but hope that it will be thus—that the voice of one who will cry, "Thus saith the Lord, . . ." will never be missing from our midst. We can only hope that such a voice will yet resound, not to be silenced by fear, personal interests, or betrayal.

A prophet like Archbishop Romero is a gift from God. We cannot "schedule" such a gift in our lives and history. But our nation, and our church, must not allow his voice, or that of other prophets, to fall silent. Were this to come to pass, the terrible prophecy of Amos would be fulfilled:

> Yes, days are coming, says the Lord God,
>   when I will send famine upon the land:
> Not a famine of bread, or thirst for water,
>   but for hearing the word of the Lord.
> Then shall they wander from sea to sea
> and rove from the north to the east,
>   but they shall not find it [Amos 8:11–12].

Let us hope, rather, that this will not come to pass—that men and women of good will, and the church in our land, will hear the word of the Lord, which, while it is a word of denunciation, is a word of orientation and encouragement, as well. Let us hope that Archbishop Romero's prophetic word will live on. Bishop Pedro Casaldáliga called Archbishop Romero's martyrdom "his finest homily." And he concluded:

> Saint Romero of the Americas,
> our shepherd and our martyr,
> none shall ever still
> that last homily!

November, 1980

CHAPTER 4

Archbishop Romero's Meaning
for Theology*

By way of a preliminary approach to the subject of the meaning of Archbishop Romero for theology, we need only recall that Archbishop Romero was himself a person of profound, powerful theological thought, and that it was in function of this thought that he built up the mission of the evangelization of his archdiocese and the church of the poor there. Archbishop Romero developed a prodigious theological reflection on the faith, and expressed that reflection in scores of homilies, addresses, and pastoral letters.

Familiar as he was with the theology of Vatican II, Archbishop Romero's theological thought gradually took on a concretion in terms of the intuitions of Medellín and Puebla, and eventually centered on the basic elements of these intuitions: an integral liberation of Christians and other human beings from every kind of slavery, and the preferential option of the church for the poor. Surely we may say of his theology what he himself said of his church. Archbishop Romero said that his was "a church whose only desire has been to live, in sincerity of heart, the mission of that servant of Yahweh 'sent to announce the

---

*On March 22, 1985, the Universidad Centroamericana José Simeón Cañas conferred upon Archbishop Romero a doctorate in theology, *honoris causa*. The present work is an address delivered on that occasion. It was originally published as "El significado de Monseñor Romero para la teología," *Estudios Centroamericanos*, March 1985, pp. 155–66.

good news to the poor, to heal the brokenhearted, to proclaim liberty to captives and those deprived of their freedom, to console all who weep' " (Georgetown address, February 14, 1978).[8] Archbishop Romero's theology was a liberation theology in the most precise evangelical and historical meaning of the term: a Christian theology, based on God's revelation and on the tradition and magisterium of the church, and an authentic Latin American theology, which always refers to and responds to the sufferings and hopes of our crucified peoples.

There can be no doubt, then, that Archbishop Romero was a profound theologian. He was not, of course, a professional theologian. He was a pastor, and the theology he developed was more biblical and pastoral than speculative. And yet that theology, from its point of departure in the concrete realities of El Salvador, actually advanced the theological intuitions of Medellín and Puebla. Many theologians have acknowledged this, and they demonstrate their acknowledgment by their numerous citations of his writings in their own.

Archbishop Romero as a Theological Event: Word of God and Word of the People of God

While all of this is important, we still have not plumbed the depths of Archbishop Romero's significance for theology. This significance transcends his particular theology, and is to be sought in his entire reality—in his thought and in his ministry, in his life and in his martyrdom. Theology, after all, however it may be defined, is always an attempt to explicitate and unify two fundamental dimensions of Christian faith. It sees our history from the standpoint of God, and sees God from the standpoint of our history; and then it seeks to act upon history from the standpoint of God, and to correspond to God from the standpoint of history.

But if theology is to be able to perform this task, something must occur in history—something very important. There must be "theological events" in history. These are persons and peoples in whom, in one and the same movement, appear the word of God and the word of the people of God, both appearing in the present, although both must be seen through the lens of past revelation. Only thus can there be a theology of and for the present, a theology that will unify both of these words — something theology does not often do. A theology that neglects the word of God's people will risk becoming a reflection on God in isolation from any praxis of historical response to God; and a theology that neglects the word of God will run the risk of reflecting on this praxis without any appreciation of its gratuity.

Such a theological event was Archbishop Romero: the current, unified word of God and of God's people. Hence his enormous significance for Christian faith, for the church, and for the Salvadoran people. Archbishop Romero rendered God and God's people present to theology, and taught theology to speak of God and God's people in a Christian fashion.

It should cause no astonishment that we speak of Archbishop Romero as the *word of God* for El Salvador. The God of Christian faith is not a universal, timeless Idea; nor again an amorphous Force homogeneously present to — or absent from — all aspects of human history. Our God is a God who seeks out individuals and peoples with a word that is at once divine and concrete. Through Abraham, Moses, and the prophets, God pronounced the divine word of promise and liberation, a word of denunciation and consolation. In the divine Son, Jesus Christ, God has pronounced the definitive word of absolute nearness to us, the word of our salvation. But not even with the coming of Christ has the divine word fallen silent in this world: the divine Spirit continues to raise up vessels of the word of God, thereby leading us to truth and salvation, throughout the whole of history.

This is what has occurred with Archbishop Romero. In him, God both has spoken, proclaiming the divine word of protest and denunciation amidst the oppressed and hopeful Salvadoran people, and has fallen silent before such abominations as may be beheld here. And withal, through Archbishop Romero God has proclaimed the word of promise, of justice, and of the defense and consolation of the oppressed.

Archbishop Romero was conscious of being a vessel of God's word, at least in the sense of desiring that his word be God's word. And so in solemn, important moments he spoke explicitly "in the name of God," as when, in his last Sunday homily, he demanded: "Stop the repression!" (March 23, 1980). He always desired that God become present through his own word. "I have earnestly sought of the Lord that this poor word ... not be a word of human eloquence or wisdom, but that my person and accent be lost" (April 12, 1979). Or again: "I make no other claim than that of being a simple preacher of the word of God" (December 3, 1978).

It is not easy for a human word to refer to God. But this is how the Salvadoran people understood the word of Archbishop Romero, and not only in what he said, but in how he said it. Archbishop Romero spoke words of truth—the whole truth. "In my luggage I have no contraband and no lies—only truth," he said on his return from Puebla (February 18, 1979). This truth was a truth of his own, surely, and this is why he was so eager to be informed about the problems around him, and why he analyzed them. This truth was the one he presented in his homilies and addressed through argumentation and reasoning. But above all, the truth he proclaimed in his word was a self-evident one, a truth that springs from the very heart of reality, one that has no need of justifying itself before human beings but rather requires that human beings justify themselves before it—a truth larger than our partial truths, a truth that makes these truths possible and judges them, while ever demanding that we human beings seek the truth personally.

Furthermore, Archbishop Romero pronounced his word with great credibility. The Salvadoran people grasped that his person was lost behind his word—that he never pronounced this word in function of any personal or institutional interests of his own, that he never whittled down or manipulated this word, that he never told half-truths, or cautious truths, or propagandistic truths, that he never fled the grave risks entailed in pronouncing this word. "If it is really God's word, it can explode, and not many are willing to carry it. If it were defused, no one would be afraid to" (September 9, 1979). Archbishop Romero was not only a preacher of the word of truth, but a bearer of the same, with all its weight. It was not he who had the word, but the word that possessed him. It filled him with joy, yes, but it annihilated him, as well. For it required the surrender of his very life.

The radical truth of the word that Archbishop Romero pronounced, and the credibility with which he pronounced it, in a land where truth does not reign, demonstrated that there is such a thing as truth after all. ("Truth is missing from our environment," he said [April 12, 1979]. "There are more than enough pens for hire and words for sale" [February 18, 1979].) And by recommending that truth to his listeners, he rendered the God of truth present in our society.

We see this most clearly in his word of denunciation, his word of defense of the poor: "The service of human dignity and its defense, the suffering and humiliation of countless human beings, the outrage and abandonment of so many families—all this has wrenched from our church an anguished cry of denunciation and repudiation" (Georgetown address). And with this cry of denunciation and repudiation on the lips of Archbishop Romero himself, the people could only believe that it was God's own cry. "This is the empire of hell!" he exclaimed, summing up the situation in his country—and the people concluded that this was the very judgment of God (June 24, 1979). But they believed the same thing when he dared to assert that, despite all, salvation was possible. While this prophet's lamentations were steeped in pain, and his denunciations rang with thunder and threat, his last word was always a promise of hope. "In the fullness of hope and faith—and not only divine faith, but human faith as well—believing not only in God but in human beings, too—I say to you: Yes, there is a solution!" (February 18, 1979). There is a way out of this hell. There is a way to salvation. Daring as these words may be, more daring still is the deep conviction (and not merely the orthodox, routine repetition) that God is salvation, and that therefore hope is truer than despair and more prudent than acceptance and resignation. Archbishop Romero believed that God is salvation, but he could communicate his belief only because his whole life and death were filled with love, were in the service of love. In life he loved his people without counting the cost: "I shall not abandon my people. In their company I shall run every risk my ministry calls for" (November 11, 1979). And he understood his impending death as the ultimate act of love: "I shall be offering my blood for the redemption and resurrection of El Salvador. . . . May my blood be the seed of liberty, and a sign of the hope that will soon become a reality" (interview in *Excelsior* [Mexico City], March 1980). And in saying this he communicated to others his sacred conviction that love is truly the ultimate reality, that which must be accomplished and received at all cost, that which demands immense sacrifices but which also promises—without explaining it—salvation. In his word, Archbishop Romero communicated his conviction that love sends us straight to God, since God is love.

In Archbishop Romero, the Salvadoran people came to know more of God than they ever had known before, for God had drawn near to them in this human being. And in Archbishop Romero, theology was enabled to develop the mysterious reality of God in a more Christian fashion. Now theology came to know more of the truth and love of God than it had ever known before in El Salvador, for Archbishop Romero told the truth and only the truth, and loved and only loved. This is what we mean when we say that Archbishop Romero was the word of God.

But he was the *word of the people of God,* as well—an aspect of which theology customarily takes less account. "These homilies are meant to be the voice of this people. They are meant to be the voice of the voiceless" (July 29, 1977). In Archbishop Romero the word of the Salvadoran people came to expression first of all as a deafening cry: the wail of the orphans, the pain of the tortured, the silence of the murdered, the anguish of the persecuted, the tragedy of the *campesinos,* the misery of the slum-dwellers, the agony of a people. But he interpreted this cry of theirs not only as a political outcry, a human protest, but as the word of the people addressed to God, as well. Hence he pronounced his word not only in the name of God, but also "in the name of this suffering people, whose screams and cries mount to heaven, and daily grow louder" (March 23, 1980).

Archbishop Romero also expressed the believing word, the Christian word of his people—their conversion, their hope, their commitment, their generous gift of themselves even unto martyrdom. With what pride he would present at Puebla this, the best of what his people had to give: "I am excited, dear brothers and sisters. I am going to Puebla, and I am going to take with me, in my voice, . . . the expression of this church that you are. You! What a living church! What a martyred church! How filled with the Holy Spirit! . . . May my humble voice at Puebla be the echo of the voice of all of these communities of yours" (December 31, 1978). And with what perceptivity he could make the most terrible statements: "I rejoice, brothers and sisters, that our church is persecuted precisely for its preferential option for the poor, and for its attempt to incarnate the interest of the poor" (July 15, 1979). His word, then, was the voice of the best that the people of God had to offer.

But Archbishop Romero believed further that God receives a response not only from the people of God as a church, but also from all who lovingly respond to the dictates of their conscience with love for their sisters and brothers, whether or not they know that this is a response to God as well. With theological depth, and exquisite delicacy, he had the courage to assert:

> The activity performed in human beings by the Spirit that raised Jesus from the dead is bigger than the church. A great part of Christ's redemptive power lies beyond the frontiers of the church; and the liberative activities of individuals and groups, even of those not professedly Christian, are set in motion by the Spirit of Jesus [Third Pastoral Letter].

In his address at Georgetown University, Archbishop Romero insisted that he was accepting an honorary doctorate from the institution not only in the name of his church, but also in that of "other men and women of good will who have embodied, incarnated, this cause, and who have defended it with the heroism of the very blood of martyrs." Thus he understood his word to be actually that of the whole Salvadoran people, the word of the suffering of all of them without exception, and of their whole generous response to God in their love for their sisters and brothers.

With Archbishop Romero, the Salvadoran people learned a better way to respond to God, and, in addition, learned the theology of a theoretical development of their response. But all of this could occur only because, like Christ, Archbishop Romero was transformed into the word of his people, as he emptied himself, condescended (in the best sense of the word) to the level of the poor and the small, and then responded to God personally, from the midst of this freely accepted poverty, oppression, and death. This is why the people regarded him as their brother, as someone terribly close to them. Archbishop Romero was their actual representative before God, a fellow human of theirs who nevertheless could present God with their own word, the word with which they wished to respond to that God. This is what we mean when we say that Archbishop Romero was the word of the people of God.

Finally, in all of this, Archbishop Romero was a *theological event.* Paraphrasing the prologue to the Gospel of John, we may say that, in his three years at the head of our local church, Archbishop Romero made the Word of God dwell among Salvadorans—made that Word to "pitch his tent" (John 1:14) among the poor, the *campesinos,* the tortured, the imprisoned, the orphans and widows, the slain. With him the Word of God drew near all of our people, in compassion for the oppressed, in menace for the mighty. With him the word of God became "sharper than any two-edged sword, piercing the depths of hearts" and history, dividing human beings and setting them in confrontation, but this word was also accepted by those who love justice and truth. And to paraphrase the Letter to the Hebrews, we may say that with Archbishop Romero the word of Salvadorans mounted to heaven—their tears and their groans, and, yes, their obedience. The cries of a whole people were transformed into the prayer Archbishop Romero offered to God. But with him as well, mercy and fidelity, love and the blood of martyrs that so abundantly bathes our earth, mounted to God, the agreeable offering of an innocent victim and the ultimate response to God's love: love for one's brothers and sisters.

Archbishop Romero as Inspiration for Theology

Such theological events are the very life of theology. They are essential—although not altogether sufficient—for a rediscovery of the origin of theology in revelation, as well as for an adequate orientation of theology throughout the course of history. Archbishop Romero himself found the inspiration for "his" theology in what he understood to be theological events: the presence of God in the poor, and the faith of the poor and the martyrs. What Archbishop Romero was in the totality of his life, this he taught theology to utter. Basically, he taught theology to speak of God and the poor in one breath. He taught it to speak of the God *of* the poor, and he taught it *how* to speak of God and the poor.

God of the Poor

Archbishop Romero was a source of inspiration with respect to a number of different elements in the content of theology. But let us concentrate on the content of theology *per antonomasiam:* God.

For Archbishop Romero, God was the God of Jesus Christ, in all of the fullness of the biblical revelation of this mystery. But precisely because God is the God of Jesus Christ, this God is a partisan God—a God who shows partiality. This God appears in a primordial correlation with the poor of this world. The good news is for the poor. The Reign of God is for the poor. Puebla says it admirably: Simply by virtue of the fact that they are poor, "God takes up their defense and loves them" (Puebla Final Document, no. 1142). And by virtue of being a God of the poor, God comes forward with a salvific will in their regard. God makes a gift of self to them, by offering them a Reign, and again by coming forward as the just Sovereign who is bent on doing them justice in a spirit of partiality.

Archbishop Romero had a profound grasp of the necessary identity between the God of Jesus Christ and the God of the poor, and he drew the ineluctable conclusions. The prime attribute of poverty as experienced in our lands is its kinship with death—the slow, sure death produced by unjust structures, and the violent, repressive death inflicted on those who seek, in all justice and right, to shake off the chains of poverty. Immersed in this death, Archbishop Romero affirmed that life is the prime mediation between God and creatures, and the primary criterion for the discernment of the authenticity of faith in God. Faith in God is an urgent affair. And the primary aspect of its urgency is its requirement that the believer make an either/or choice between life and death—between the God of life and the idols

of death. Belief in God entails, first and foremost, the fostering
of the life of the poor.

Life is not everything. But Archbishop Romero solemnly asserted that in circumstances where life is so precarious, so
threatened and crushed, one cannot believe in God without defending life, and this is God's primary message to us. "There is
nothing so important for the church as human life, . . . especially
in the person of the poor and oppressed" (March 16, 1980). Or
again: "God did not make death, nor is God entertained at the
destruction of the living. . . . God made life, and wishes it to
subsist, and not die" (July 1, 1979).

Archbishop Romero believed in the God of life — not, however, in some abstract, universalistic way, but in a concrete, "partial" way, so that when he defended the life of the poor he
believed that he was defending God. Paraphrasing Saint Irenaeus's dictum, "The glory of God is the living person," Archbishop Romero dared to say: "The glory of God is the living
poor person" (conclusion to the Louvain address). Hence his
consistent defense of the life of the poor, and his denunciation
of assaults on that life; his demands for justice, and for radical
changes in our lethal socio-economic structures; his encouragement of the political organization of the poor; and his tireless
demand that the economy, the administration of justice, the
armed forces, education, the media, and the church itself all be
directed and organized with the life of the poor in view. There
is no "shift of the faith" in any of this. On the contrary, this is
precisely an expression of faith in the true God, the God of life.

And here theology, as well, has its first lesson to learn. In
conversation with Leonardo Boff, Archbishop Romero asked
theologians to develop a theology of life, and this from a very
precise viewpoint, which he couched in a remarkable formulation: "We must defend God's minimum gift, which is also the
maximum: the gift of life."[9] This is "back to basics," back to life,
back to something so evidently demanded by the will of God
that it presents theology with a challenge it simply may not ignore: the variety of its content must not relativize the basic
element; theological sophistication must not stifle the evident;
a hasty appeal to fullness of life must not be transformed into
an alibi for ignoring the death of the poor. Only thus will it be

possible to present a God who is the defender, vindicator, and liberator of the poor.

It was precisely through this seeming minimum, the life of the poor, and in no way apart from it, that Archbishop Romero presented God as fullness, as well. Irenaeus continues the statement cited above with the following words: "And the life of the human being is the vision of God" (see Romero's homily of February 10, 1980), and Archbishop Romero truly believed that the God of Jesus came to bring life and bring it in abundance (John 10:10). God is revealed as the defender of the minimum, but also as the humanizer of human beings as peoples, and the One who draws them to fullness. Archbishop Romero spoke of both—minimal life, and full humanization—with conviction and credibility. The word he pronounced on the fullness of God had nothing of the routine, the disincarnate, the alienating about it. He never spoke of the fullness of God in dissociation from the life of the poor. He never flagged in his denunciations of injustice, poverty, and death as intolerable in the eyes of God. "This blood, this death, touch the very heart of God" (March 16, 1980).

But he also presented God as the Father of Jesus. God is like a good mother, who is close to her little ones. In God are repose, peace, and joy, to be discovered there by life's afflicted, society's marginalized, and those a smug piety sneers at. When he had nothing else to offer the poor, he offered them God's love. One Christmas Eve he said:

> Ah, that my voice could come to all shut-ins, like a ray of light, a ray of Christmas hope, to tell you, too, the sick and elderly of Sarah House, you who are sick in this hospital and all hospitals, you in the urban slums and gullies, you the coffee cutters trying to earn enough in one short season to live for the whole year, you the victims of torture—to tell you, too, that the eternal counsel of God has taken thought of you all [December 24, 1978].

Amidst the terrible poverty of our land, and with a call to fight that poverty, Archbishop Romero presented God as the One who guarantees the dignity of the poor—the dignity of a people of the poor. Archbishop Romero presented God in terms of the possibility of living humanely in midst of dehumanization. He encouraged the poor to live poverty in the spirit of the Beatitudes, with a pure heart, with bowels of mercy, with fortitude in persecution, with universal solidarity, and thus to become the daughters and sons of God. In recognizing their objective theological dignity, he restored to them their historical dignity. With Archbishop Romero the poor began to understand their history in terms of a contrast, the contrast between once upon a time and now: "Once we were nonpersons, and a nonpeople; now we are persons, and a people." It was this fullness, this divine plenitude, that formed the basis of Archbishop Romero's presentation of God.

Further: Archbishop Romero believed that God is the humanizing element not only of persons, but of history. With God, we move out more rapidly and more authentically toward our own fulfillment. Archbishop Romero presented God as the God of utopia. In a striking statement of the one advantage of Christian labors for a social utopia over non-Christian labors for the same end—the advantage of toiling precisely for the Reign of God—he declared: "The Church contributes only one value: a sure hope" (February 14, 1979). Thereby he affirmed that he believed in the future, and in a good, salvific future—God's future. The God of utopia never finds full correspondence in history. But that God draws history forward that it may give more of itself, and inspires all social processes to move in the direction of justice, peace, and a communion of sisters and brothers. The God of utopia corrects any deviations from this path. Archbishop Romero believed that, by keeping God's utopia alive, by keeping faith with the invitation that comes from above and from the future, one may always find the right direction in which to move to construct history. Only thus, he held, do we generate the values we need to build that history in a human and humane way. Only thus can we overcome human *hybris,* with its tendency to absolutize—and thereby pervert—its achievements. Only thus shall we be able to maintain a simultaneity and dynamic equilibrium otherwise so rarely attained in history: between justice and freedom, struggle and reconciliation, realism and hope.

God's utopia—so intangible, so vulnerable—is the "historical reserve" that Archbishop Romero offered, on which we may ever seize in order to recover hope, in order to put our hand to the task of forging justice, in order to strive, ever and again, to keep justice from spoiling, to keep it from going bad, to keep it in good condition and even to improve it. It is this utopia, taken seriously, and with an effort to put it in practice, that makes men and women be, as Archbishop Romero called them, "forgers of history" (November 11, 1979).

This God of life, our divine Parent ever near, this Utopia of all fullness, was the content of Archbishop Romero's theology, preaching, and activity. This is the God with whom the prophet Micah begs us to walk humbly through history toward transcendence. And this, finally, is what Archbishop Romero tells us about God: that God is transcendent mystery. "Those who do not understand transcendence do not understand us," he said (February 2, 1979). "A transcendent salvation is necessary" (January 7, 1979).

But precisely on the strength of his concern to proclaim the transcendence of the God of Jesus Christ and not of some other divinity, Archbishop Romero was supremely careful to present the transcendence of God in a Christian manner. To those who appealed to it hastily and without regard for its incarnation among us, he said: "The transcendent is not enough. How nice, to be able to write about the transcendent, and to have to speak of nothing else!" (September 9, 1979). He correctly understood the transcendence of God as the difference between "God's majesty and our littleness" (February 10, 1980). At the same time he presented it, correctly, as something present in history precisely as greater than history. With the evangelical intuition so characteristic of him, he identified this historical transcendence as the challenge to respond and correspond to the God who becomes present in history, and he did so just as Jesus did in Matthew 25, on the Last Judgment. Archbishop Romero stated: "If we concern ourselves with the interests of the poor and helpless, these 'least ones'—and not because of some general humanitarian attitude or other, but precisely because they represent Jesus to a faith that reveals the true identity of the lowly, the marginalized, the poor, the sick—if we see Jesus in them, this is transcendence" (September 30, 1979).

Thus an approach to God from the dialectical unification of the smallest and greatest, of life and the fullness of life, of history and transcendence, is, we should venture to say, Archbishop Romero's most significant contribution to theology. In approaching the transcendent mystery of God from the basic reality of the cries and hopes of the poor, Archbishop Romero has furnished us with a better knowledge of God as the transcendent "ever greater" God—the *Deus semper major* of creation, of divine parenthood, of liberation, and of utopia—who is precisely the immanent "ever lesser" God at the same time—the *Deus semper minor* concealed in poverty and annihilated in crucifixions. In the same movement, he has also made a contribution to the development of a christology (in the concrete reality of Christ, one sees God) and an ecclesiology based on faith in this God and the following of this Christ. He has helped our theological understanding of faith as our total response and surrender to the God of the poor.

The Christian Theological Task: From the Midst of the Poor, and for the Poor

Archbishop Romero was a great inspiration for theological content, then. But he also made an important contribution to theological method. He showed us how to practice theology precisely in Christian fashion. First and foremost, he showed us the *locus from which* theology must be practiced.

Where one seeks God is not a matter for indifference. God is to be sought not necessarily where we, or theology, might like to see God manifested, but where God has promised to be manifested: in the poor of this world. And a Christian theology must develop the human being's response to God not from just any random starting point, but from the starting point of the gospel: in the discipleship of Jesus poor and crucified, and in the response of the poor who "have understood the mysteries of the Reign."

Archbishop Romero found God in the poor, hidden in their crosses and their limitations, and manifested in their conversion, their hope, their unreserved commitment. None of this rendered

Scripture or the tradition of the church superfluous for his faith and his own theological reflection, or tempted him to undervalue the permanent magisterium of the church—whose zealous student and loyal disciple, on the contrary, he ever remained. But none of the latter, in turn, deprived the poor of their decisive importance as locus of faith, the church, and theology. "It is in this world without a human face, this sacrament of the Suffering Servant of Yahweh today, that the church in my archdiocese has sought to achieve incarnation" (Louvain address).

At the same time—to return to content for a moment—"basic points of faith have been enriched through his incarnation in reality" (ibid.). What are sin and grace? What is love, and its necessary concretion in justice? What are historical hope and transcendent hope? What is faith in God and in the Christ of God? The answers to all of these questions have been enriched, as Archbishop Romero put it, through the church's incarnation in the poor.

And this is the second great lesson Archbishop Romero holds for theology. That discipline must be practiced from the midst of the poor *as poor,* from among the poor *as a people of the poor.* The *people* of God, constituted in its vast majority by the poor, are the primary recipients of the revelation of God, and the primary subjects of a response to that revelation, as Vatican II teaches. Inescapably, then, theology must refer to this people as such in order to have a valid point of departure. But as the people *of the poor,* the people of God also have an "evangelizing potential"—as Puebla says (Puebla Final Document, no. 1147). Accordingly, theology must refer to the poor not only formally, but for the sake of its very content. The poor obviously do not enable the theologian to develop all of the functions of theology, nor can popular theological reflection ever replace that of technical theology. But the poor provide the theologian with the only adequate point of departure for technical theology. That is, they provide technical theology with its foundation: an authentic reading of the gospel of Jesus, whose privileged addressees are the poor themselves, and a knowledge of the basic truth of history, which they express better than anyone else because they suffer more than anyone else; of course theology must thereupon also analyze both the gospel and historical reality in a more technical and theoretical manner.

In his pastoral and magisterial ministry, Archbishop Romero gave us a remarkable example of how the church and theology should relate to the poor. In the first place, they should ask them questions—as Archbishop Romero himself did before going to Puebla, or while developing his Fourth Pastoral Letter—and should take their responses seriously, including "certain doctrinal and pastoral imprecisions and audacities" in these responses that "have served as a stimulus to the charism of magisterium and discernment with which the Lord has entrusted me" (Fourth Pastoral Letter). Second, the church should learn from the poor: "I believe that a bishop has much to learn from the faithful" (September 9, 1979). Third, while the church surely ought to exercise its own magisterium authoritatively, it should do so in a spirit of dialogue, especially when confronted with new problems, or new concretions of old ones: "Our limitations call for dialogue," said Archbishop Romero in his Third Pastoral Letter. And the church ought to be willing to submit its determinations to verification by the people: "Precisely in the charisms that the Spirit bestows on the people, the bishop finds the touchstone of his own authenticity" (September 9, 1979).

When we say, "from the midst of the poor," then, we are not playing with words. The expression has a precise meaning. It does not suggest a substitute for the data of past revelation; but neither is it replaceable when it comes to grasping and responding to God's manifestation in the present. Theology must be practiced from a starting point in these two poles, the same twin point of departure that Archbishop Romero required for the pastoral ministry: "Only by listening to the cry of the poor from a starting point in the data and their analysis, on the one hand, and on the other by hearing the word of Jesus and his church, shall we be able to find the solution, and the pastoral response, to any of our problems" (Third Pastoral Letter).

Theology must be biblical and ecclesial, yes. And it must be technical, yes. But it must be popular, as well. It must arise from, respond to, and subsume the reality of the people of God, and God's people of the poor.

Furthermore, like any Christian task, theology must be pervaded and carried out with a particular spirit, a Christian spirit. Theology is a human, creaturely task—open to grace, but shot through with sinfulness, as well. Although it must be performed according to the laws of all intelligence, it cannot therefore proclaim itself absolutely autonomous. Rather, it must not only yield Christian content, but it must be performed in a Christian manner, as well.

Archbishop Romero likewise exemplified, and to perfection, the *Christian quality* with which any ecclesial activity should be invested. To take a significant example, his archiepiscopal ministry had its own intrinsic structures and its specific functions, yes; but this did not of itself answer the question of how to be an archbishop in a Christian way. And to be Christian, to do things in a Christian manner, is the ideal of theology, as well.

The first requisite of the theological undertaking, then, is that it be open to *conversion.* Theology can be the vehicle of sin. This can produce alienation. Theology can "put the people to sleep" (December 9, 1979). Theology can "fail to tell the truth when it ought to tell it" (December 31, 1978). Theology can be "indifferent to the poor" (July 1, 1979). Yes, theology is capable of committing all of these sins. Theology, too, can become that "static Christianity that reminds you of a museum" (June 21, 1979). Of course, as Archbishop Romero insisted, all of these dangers threaten the whole area of the religious, and not just theology.

Therefore theology must be open to conversion and verification. It must examine its conscience. It must take a long, hard look at its subjective interests and objective relevance. Is it perchance maintaining itself voluntaristically, when it is no longer of any help to any one? Worse still, might it be being transformed into an ideological support for sinful interests and structures?

The theological task is one of *service.* Before all else, theology should address the concrete problems of the people of God, however new and objectively difficult these may be, and notwithstanding a certain intellectual helplessness before their novelty and gravity. Theology must not maintain an a priori agenda. Archbishop Romero said: "We are the people's shepherds, and we have the duty to furnish them with a Christian and ecclesial

answer to the problems that unsettle so many of their con-
sciences" (Third Pastoral Letter). This is what theology, too,
ought to be doing. To be sure, it also pertains to its ministry of
service to place concrete problems against a broader theoretical
horizon, to foresee future directions for ecclesial situations, to
interrelate current problems with the data of revelation, and so
on. In other words, theology has no business becoming an "answer" to problems in a spirit of immediatism, or interim "cop-
ing." It must maintain its systematic character. But this is no
excuse for ignoring the nature of the theological task as one of
service. Theology must place itself at the service of the actual
questions of history, the actual problems of the people of God.
It must not do precisely the opposite: it must not regard these
problems merely as material for its own development as theology. Nor of course must it allow itself to ignore problems simply
because it does not know their solutions.

Theology must be a serious attempt to be *effective*. It must
actually attempt to solve the great problems of life and death,
of humanization and dehumanization. Of its very nature, the
theological enterprise comports the duty to seek the greatest
possible accumulation of usable knowledge, in the form not only
of theological analyses, but of social, economic, and political
analyses, as well. It should encourage the realization of what it
proposes. It should assist a lucid practice, that the Reign of God
may actually come, in history. On an individual level, it should
provide the light and indicate pathways to a personal encounter
with God. Archbishop Romero gave us a working example of all
of this in the preparation of his homilies and pastoral letters.
He gave us this example in the means he took to achieve the
ends for which he strove, and he called on others to do likewise,
provided only their ends pertained to the following of Jesus, the
struggle for justice, the organization of the people; and he defined the finality of all of his activity as "doing the work of the
church in order to build the Reign of God" (December 3, 1978).

Theology must be *prepared to accept conflict and persecution.*
This is true of any Christian task, but it is especially true when
that task is directly concerned with the word of God. Archbishop
Romero had no need of being reminded of this. Both conflict
and persecution were an everyday affair with him. We need add

only that if theology seeks to be a ministry of service, and an effective one, then it will have to reckon with "a society that rejects the word of the gospel when it constitutes an obstacle to its injustice" (July 8, 1979). Theology will be accused of ignorance, heresy, Marxism, every straw at which the status quo can grasp in order to convey an impression of rationality (ibid.). When will persecution befall theology? At the moment of its most authentic explanation of the word of God. "My only comfort," Archbishop Romero said, reflecting on this tragic paradox, "is that Christ, who had sought to communicate this great truth, was likewise misunderstood, labeled rebellious, and sentenced to death, as I have received death threats during these past days" (June 3, 1979).

Finally, as the practice of theology is a gift of grace, of *gratuity*, it must steep itself in *humility* and *gratitude*. Theology has not discovered its object, or even rediscovered it, through the functioning of its own mechanisms. Rather, a piece of good news has been given to it to communicate. And this good news has been given to it, historically and concretely, by the poor. But theology should also be a thing of *joy*, as well. The truth upon which theology bears is not just any random truth, but ultimately a truth that is good news. Theology must therefore be profoundly evangelical, in the original sense of the word. Archbishop Romero never failed to communicate this. "I simply wish to be the builder of a great assertion: the assertion of God, who loves us and wants to save us" (February 25, 1979).

Oscar Arnulfo Romero: Legacy and Future

Theology is indebted to Archbishop Romero's inspiration for a great many other things besides those considered in this presentation. But perhaps what I have said will be sufficient to convey a somewhat better appreciation of the fact that Archbishop Romero was himself a theological thinker, and that, above all, he was a theology-inspiring event. As to the former, here was a *homo doctus,* a learned person, who knew and practiced theology. As to the latter, he was an authentic *doctor,* who taught by inspiring, and who inspired by teaching. In order to appreciate Archbishop Romero's legacy to theology, we need only to come to appreciate these two elements in conjunction.

The future of his legacy cannot be forecast. We do not know the future. But let me put forward a pair of considerations that might shed some light on what is likely to occur. First, it has now been over a decade since the martyrdom of Archbishop Romero, and far from disappearing, his word and work have actually grown in meaningfulness and influence. This fact is inescapable. This legacy surely has a future. Second, a process receives its sense and meaning from its term, and Archbishop Romero's end was not an ordinary death: it was a martyrdom, and it now becomes the hermeneutic principle for an interpretation of his word — not only by virtue of the subjective credibility it confers on that word, but by virtue of the truth with which it objectively sanctions that word. Martyrdom is no accident in El Salvador. It is the unequivocal sign of the presence of truth. And the dimensions of the martyrdom are an index of the magnitude of the truth. Because the dimensions of the martyrdom of Archbishop Romero of San Salvador, who had been honored with so many degrees and awards, and who was a Nobel Peace Prize nominee, were so great — then the truth he offered us must have been great indeed.

I doubt that it would be an exaggeration to say that, with the passing of time, Archbishop Romero will become, in fact is already becoming, one of the great doctors of the church — indeed, one of the Fathers of the Church, several of whom, like himself, were bishops and martyrs as well as individuals who joined, in their persons, a creative pastoral mission, great holiness, and profound theological thought. It was these Fathers of the Church, holy and wise, who stimulated and shaped the living tradition of that church, and whom the passage of the years has only rendered still more current and inspiring as symbols of the great moments of the church.

Archbishop Romero is becoming one of these great moments of the church — a pillar of faith and an inspiration for theology. Situations will change, and some of the things he said will become obsolete. But the deeper meaning of the things he said will forever abide in the church of El Salvador and the church universal.

Archbishop Romero, too, thought about the future. He

thought, first of all, about the future of his people: "The liberation cry of this people is a cry that ascends to God, and there
is nothing, there is no one, that can hold it back any longer"
(January 27, 1980). He thought about their hope: "Christ will
make this sun to shine that is the *campesino*. . . . He wants it to
shine, this sun of justice and truth" (July 29, 1979). And, citing
the prophecy: "Upon these ruins will shine the glory of the
Lord" (January 7, 1979).

He reflected on his own future, as well. His doom grew more
imminent with the passing days. In all humility, he said of himself: "If they kill me, I shall rise again in the Salvadoran people"
(interview in *Excelsior,* March 1980). And he reflected on his
word, that word of God and of the Salvadoran people upon
which I have commented in these pages. And he said: "The word
remains. . . . My voice will disappear. But my word, which is
Christ, will abide in the hearts of those who have been willing
to receive it" (December 17, 1978).

What he said of himself, in such humility, has come true. His
word remains. Those who make an attempt to live as responsible
human beings in this crucified, hope-filled Latin America of
ours, can always turn to him. Those who seek to live their faith,
their hope, and their commitment in this church of ours, will
always find inspiration and encouragement in Archbishop Romero. Those who wish to practice theology responsibly on this
continent of ours, will ever find inspiration in his word and his
life.

PART 2

Archbishop Romero: Witness of God

CHAPTER 5

Archbishop Romero:
Of This World, and of God*

1. Three years ago today, Oscar Arnulfo Romero was felled by the assassin's bullet, spilling his blood before the altar of God. Thus he found his life fulfilled: in sharing the lot of so many Salvadorans whose death is by murder. And thus he found his priesthood fulfilled: as Jesus fulfilled his own, by offering not the blood of lambs, but his own body and his own blood. In that sacred moment, Archbishop Romero was transformed into a universal human being, a person for all ages, a symbol of the hope and tragedy of the Salvadoran people, and a witness and martyr of God's truth, justice, and love.

Today, three years later, his death and resurrection are celebrated in many parts of the world. We recall them because to recall, to remember, *recordari,* is a joy and obligation of the Christian heart. Jesus said: "Do this in memory of me," speaking of his own death. And how many millions of human beings since then, all down through history, have recalled that tragic moment of Jesus' murder, when he was violently deprived of his life by those who practiced injustice and hated the light! It is also of the greatest importance that we recall that twenty-fourth of March on which the Salvadoran people—so accustomed to tragic news, and to having death as their companion—stood

---

*Homily delivered March 24, 1983, at an ecumenical service celebrated in memory of Archbishop Romero at St. James's Church, Piccadilly, London. First published in *Estudios Centroamericanos,* March 1983, pp. 289–96.

thunderstruck at the report: Archbishop Oscar Romero, that good, that compassionate person, that defender of the poor, that voice of the voiceless, that prophet, that excoriator of oppressors, had been murdered.

It is important to remember that day because in this way we shall not forget or ignore the dark side of our human history— the cross of Jesus, the thousands, the millions who die every day, victims sacrificed to the idols of death, be those idols absolutized private property in a capitalistic society, or the national security regimes, both of which Archbishop Romero identified as the idols of El Salvador. It is important that we not forget that we human beings are capable of murdering our neighbors—Marianella García and the organizers of the Sonsonate cooperative are simply further, recent examples—capable of destroying God's creation.

At the same time, the obligation of *recordari* is a joyful one, as well. It is a source of hope. Jesus said: "Do this until I come again," and three days later was raised by his Father. Archbishop Romero said: "If they kill me, I shall rise again in the Salvadoran people," and suddenly we behold his resurrection, his presence among us. This is the meaning of today's celebration.

Archbishop Romero is present, very present. He is risen, very much risen, among the Salvadoran people, as in so many other places on this earth. His *current presence,* surely, like Jesus' presence, is a two-edged sword, dividing the human race in two. That presence brings to light both the evil deeds of the oppressor, and the good works of those who go in quest of justice and peace. It is hope for the poor, and is a threat to the mighty. Thus his presence is observable in very different, contrary ways.

There are those today who still fear Archbishop Romero— in the government, in the armed forces, in the oligarchy, and even in the hierarchy. They would like to forget him, reduce him to silence, bury his spirit along with his body. Then there are those who praise him today as a saint and prophet of the past, but who would like to bury him in the past to still the echoes of his voice. This is the only possible explanation for the fear that gripped certain Salvadoran hearts at the mere announcement that Pope John Paul II would visit Archbishop

Romero's tomb in the cathedral, or the fear occasioned by a poster showing Archbishop Romero and the Holy Father together. Archbishop Romero becomes present today, very present, in the fear felt at the very mention of his name or showing of his photograph. Out of this fear, certain persons would like to silence his name. We are reminded of the religious leaders of Israel who forbade the apostles to "speak or teach in any way in Jesus' name" (Acts 4:18).

But there are many other Christians in the world, together with other persons of good will, for whom Archbishop Romero is very present. He is present in their lives, and they desire that he continue to be. When forbidden to speak or teach in his name, they answer, with the apostles: "We cannot leave off speaking of what we have seen and heard" (Acts 4:20). This response is an expression of their responsibility, yes; but even more, it is an expression of gratitude. Many persons loved Archbishop Romero, and many love him still. When he was murdered, they wept for him as one weeps for a father or a mother. Now they speak of him out of love and gratitude. For them, Archbishop Romero is truly very present.

He is present in all of those who suffer the horrors of repression and war; in all who seek the strength to remain faithful to the poor, and to the gospel of God; in all who, the world over, have found in his words and his life the meaning of their faith, who have rediscovered their own dignity as human beings, who have made a decision to enter into solidarity with the poor of this world. He is present in so many Salvadoran *campesinos* who visit his tomb to pray to him and speak with him; in all the oppressed, in everyone in the shelters; in those who are arrested and tortured; in the mothers, wives, and children of the disappeared, who look for counsel, courage, and hope; he is present in all of those for whom survival is a daily challenge and for whom dying is an imminent fate; in those who, in the silence of their hearts, renew their daily decision to walk with a suffering people.

2. If we now wonder why Archbishop Romero is so alive and present—if we ask ourselves the secret of this person, this Christian, this archbishop—doubtless we could develop lengthy, elaborate answers to our question. But I should like to sum them

all up—from the experience of my personal contact with him—in a twin assertion. Archbishop Romero was a person of this world, and he was a person of God. He saw and loved this world with the eyes and heart of God, and learned to know and love God from out of the hopes and anguish of this world. He brought God near this world, and brought this world to God. He took God and the world absolutely seriously; and he refused to slight the importance of either of these realities in favor of the other. This, in my judgment, is what transformed him into such an exceptional human being and Christian.

a. Archbishop Romero was a person of this world. He was a person with whom anyone genuinely interested in the problems of this world could enter into easy, friendly contact. If justice and injustice, life and death, human rights, peace and conflict were genuinely important subjects to you, you got along with Archbishop Romero famously.

A genuine interest in the grave problems of humanity, a genuine involvement with these problems, is the true attitude of incarnation. Like Jesus, Archbishop Romero became incarnate in this world, took the flesh of this world. But he took not just any random flesh: he took the flesh of poverty, a flesh weak and frail, the flesh of the poor and oppressed.

This first characteristic of Archbishop Romero is a far from ordinary thing. Frequently enough, we Christians and our local churches are in danger of ignoring or watering down certain incarnations, at times even in the name of God. Not infrequently, we attempt to emerge from this world, leave this world, and especially leave the poor and weak of this world. This is not how it was with Archbishop Romero. Like Christ, Archbishop Romero became a human being of this world, and a human being of the poor. Truly he "pitched his tent among us" (John 1:14, in the Greek).

Being incarnate in the real world, Archbishop Romero discovered the deepest of this world's truths: the poverty that cries to heaven. This poverty had concrete faces, and these faces were beloved to him: children dying, *campesinos* with neither land nor rights, slum-dwellers, the tortured corpses of his people, whose only crime had been their desire to break free of poverty and oppression. This poverty has its own structural mechanisms—

unjust social, economic, and political structures—which origi-
nate it, which bring it to a head in oppression and death, and
which Archbishop Romero denounced with such forthrightness
and vigor.

These poor persons broke his heart, and the wound never
closed. The suffering of the poor cut him to the quick. He felt
the indignation of a prophet in the midst of such misery, such
injustice, such death—and such hypocrisy in justification of it
all. But the poor also won his heart forever. He felt the compassion and mercy of Jesus for them, and made of that compassion and that mercy the guiding principle of all of his activity.
Like the first Latin American bishops, those *ex officio* protectors
of the Indian, indeed like God, who is the advocate of the poor,
Archbishop Romero was the defender of the poor.

As a defender of the poor out of conviction, and not simply
in order to fulfill the mandate he had received from the church,
he made his option for the poor—for those whom God, through
the prophets, calls "my people." Week after week he denounced
the injustices and atrocities perpetrated against them, frequently
mentioning their names in order to remind us that the poor and
oppressed are actual persons of flesh and bone, sons and daughters of God whom that God knows by name. Week after week
as well, he exposed those responsible for injustice and oppression, and the selfish interests they defend, once more naming
names, that he might call for their conversion and offer them
the good news of God's love through that conversion. He also
denounced—no common thing today—the sins of the church:
our own participation in the sin of the world.

Tirelessly, with the stubbornness of hope, Archbishop Romero repeated the absolute need of justice, of radical changes and
reforms. He encouraged all, believers and nonbelievers alike, to
toil and to struggle for the justice that brings the Reign of God
closer to us. When armed conflict broke out in El Salvador, he
made every possible effort to find a solution that would bring
peace, reconciliation, and especially, justice for the poor.

Finally, Archbishop Romero was a person of this world in
that he shared the lot of his people, and the fate—slow or
quick—of so many millions of the human beings of today's humanity: death. In life he was frequently threatened and perse-

cuted, and he foresaw his own death. But none of this separated him from his people. When he was offered a security team, he replied: "The shepherd refuses all security until security is given his flock" (July 22, 1979). Finally, like so many of his people, he was murdered. His death was the sign of his utter fidelity to God, of course; but it was also the sign of his total incarnation in this world. As he himself said, a month before his death: "The church suffers the lot of the poor: persecution" (February 17, 1980).

Then he mixed his blood with all the spilled blood of El Salvador and the world. Thus Archbishop Romero was transformed into a person *of* this world, and a person of our time, for good and all. The way he lived and died transformed him into a human being *for* our time, as well. This explains his impact not only in El Salvador, nor only on Christians, but the world over, as well, and on women and men of other beliefs and ideologies. Through his Christian way of being human, he likewise showed simply what it ought to mean today to be human in our humanity. Therefore all those who "toil in such a way as to water truth, justice, love, and goodness on the earth" (March 24, 1980) — as Archbishop Romero put it, minutes before his murder — are very close to him.

b. A person of this world, Archbishop Romero was also genuinely a person of God. He believed and trusted in God. He achieved that simple, profound thing called faith. True, a priest, an archbishop, is expected to be a person of faith. But the depth of faith achieved by Archbishop Romero is not something anyone can reach automatically. And that deep faith took us by surprise. It judged us and inspired us.

Archbishop Romero's faith in God certainly never separated him from this world. On the contrary, it was precisely his God who thrust him so powerfully into this world. For Archbishop Romero it was really God who asked him the basic questions: "What have you done with your brother?" (Gen. 4:9ff.). Are you with Mary at the foot of the cross — the cross of Jesus and of all of today's crucified? But at the same time, Archbishop Romero was convinced that there was no substitute for the human encounter with God, whether that encounter be the explicit one of priestly work, or the implicit one of fidelity to the Spirit of

God beyond the frontiers of the church. "Tell me, beloved
brothers and sisters, that the fruit of today's sermon will be that
each of us will have an encounter with God! . . . No human being
has self-knowledge without having encountered God" (February
10, 1980).

The God of Archbishop Romero was surely the God of Jesus:
a God, then, who is a Father, who is good to us, and who has
good news for us; a God, especially, of the poor, one who defends them, and loves them for the sheer fact that they are poor,
who hears the cries of God's people and comes down from
heaven to deliver them; a God who loves with tender affection
everyone regarded and despised as small, weak, powerless; a
God of nearness to the poor, one who is so close to them as to
become present on the cross to show that God shares the victims' suffering, thereby making God's love credible once and for
all; a God who raises the crucified, and seals forever the cove-
nant of hope for the poor.

This is the God in whom Archbishop Romero believed. On
one occasion, in order to express God's great love, Archbishop
Romero cited St. Irenaeus's celebrated maxim: "The glory of
God is the living person." And he translated this for El Salvador
as: "The glory of God is the living poor person." God sincerely
wills life, not death. And so God takes sides. God takes sides
for life, and actively struggles against the idols of death—those
false divinities that are not only distinct from God, and hence
introduce a polytheism, but are just the opposite of the true
God. Archbishop Romero's faith in God the Father moved him
to be a servant of life, justice, peace, and hope. But in achieving
this deep, profound faith, he showed God's love. He brought
God exceedingly close to us.

On the other hand, his faith in a God who is a parent to us
did not cause him to forget that this divine parent continues to
be God, greater than all else, greater than our very selves,
greater than our churches, greater than our hopes, greater even
than our good works, and greater, surely, than any idea we may
have of God. Here is a God who must ever be sought, however
much one may already have found God; and whose will must
always be discerned, despite what we know of God through revelation in the past, through the teachings of the church, and

through the various theologies. Here is a God, when all is said and done, whose Spirit "breathes where it will," and not necessarily where we have been expecting.

Archbishop Romero's faith in that God meant for him, *personally,* that he had ever to learn of God anew and that he had constantly to learn to believe in God. It meant that he had ever and again to ask himself the will of God in new situations of poverty, conflict, repression, and political organization on the part of Christians; he had continually to discern the will of God as regarded the social and political implications of his own activity and that of the church, and as regarded the new theological tendencies. In sum, his faith in God meant that he ever and again had to ask himself about the will of God in all the concrete situations of those new signs of the times so beautifully formulated at Medellín: a misery that cries to heaven, and longings for liberation.

It also meant, frequently enough, that he stood before God alone, with groans like those of Jesus (Heb. 5:7), asking for a communication of the divine will and the strength to carry it out. It meant frequently standing alone in the institutional church, misinterpreted or attacked even by some of his fellow bishops.

It meant, finally, feeling ultimately sent by God, and responsible to God alone, and therefore having to speak in the name of God. It was not merely a desire to stamp his words with rhetorical force, then, but an awareness, a conviction, of his responsibility before God, that moved him to say: "In the name of God, then, and in the name of this suffering people, whose screams and cries mount to heaven, and daily grow louder, I beg you, I entreat you, I order you in the name of God: Stop the repression!" (March 23, 1980).

Where human *structures* are concerned, faith in this God meant that Archbishop Romero never equated any concrete human project with the plenitude of the Reign of God. Not that he therefore relativized all of these projects equally—that of the oligarchy, that of the government, and that of the popular organizations. But he judged them all on the criterion of their distance from the Reign of God. Accordingly, while emphatically condemning the oligarchical and governmental projects, he

also criticized the errors and shortcomings of the popular project—not because he was shocked at the inevitability of human
errors in that project, but lest these errors be ignored or dissi-
mulated on principle. It was faith in the absolute truth of God
that led Archbishop Romero to discover these shortcomings and
to criticize them.

But the ultimate effect of his faith was not only that it judged
us all, and discovered our sins—which of course it did, and
continues to do—but that the God of that faith inspires us to
overcome our sins, constantly setting before our eyes the goal
of the ideal. Archbishop Romero believed that any genuine utopia will have its source in God, and that for this reason a genuine
utopia, however unattainable in history in its quality of perfection, will nevertheless contain its own power of *partial and incomplete* self-attainment in history. For Archbishop Romero,
God was the source of justice, truth, and the Reign; as well as
the font of peace, mercy, and reconciliation. How difficult, if
not impossible, we find it to strive for each of these things sep-
arately, let alone in conjunction! But Archbishop Romero never
despaired or yielded in his strivings to perform the utopian task
of humanizing history and its inhabitants through his faith in
God. It was his unshakable belief that the history of human
beings is better humanized, becomes more humane, with God,
and that when they let God be God, the men and women of this
world better attain their vocation and carry out their responsibility—that with God the meaning of their lives is enhanced and
the joy of belonging to this humanity is increased.

This is what we mean when we say that Archbishop Romero
believed in God. We are saying more than that he was a profoundly devout human being, priest, and hierarch. We are saying
more than that he was, so to speak, an expert, a professional,
on religious matters. We are saying more than that he performed
his archiepiscopal ministry to perfection. On a deeper level, we
are saying that for him God was a living reality, in whom he
trusted completely as in a parent, and whom he always obeyed
as God. Just as for Jesus, God for Archbishop Romero was the
origin of all inspiration and motivation, and the goal and ideal
of his longing. Standing resolutely between that origin and that
goal, he spent three years doing good, walking humbly with the

poor and with God (see Mic. 6:8), and offering his life to God in behalf of the poor.

3. This, in my opinion, is what Archbishop Romero was. Surely many other things could and should be said of him. I might mention his leadership in the church and nation, his many visits to the base communities, his pastoral and theological teaching, his effective approach to recovering the poor for the church and installing them there as a central element, or the impact that his ministry had beyond El Salvador and Central America. I could mention his novel, affectionate, and critical accompaniment of the popular processes, his presence in all of the conflicts, great and small, social and political, that were waged during his three years as archbishop. I could mention so much more. After all, in his case too, just as with Jesus, "if all the things he did were to be written about in detail, I doubt there would be room enough in the entire world to hold the books to record them" (John 21:25).

In my attempt to express what Archbishop Romero was as compendiously as I possibly could, I have decided to say simply that he was a person of this world and a person of God—as the great saints were, and as Jesus was, in whom was accomplished the miracle of the absolute union of world and God. It is this unification without identification that made Archbishop Romero exceptional. Through him, the gospel was transformed into a word of good news to the poor, and a word of demand upon the mighty. Through this person of this world and for this time, the gospel once again became a gospel for our times, and showed that it is indeed a gospel for all times.

If I may be allowed to conclude on just one autobiographical note, I should like to add that, for me as for so many others, it was Archbishop Romero who "showed forth the gospel with power." It was he through whom the gospel became strength for us, who called us forth from our homes, our established places in the religious life, the priesthood, or theology, and bade us walk toward unknown destinations, while we knew that we walked with and toward God. Those who wish to explain Archbishop Romero without following in his footsteps have said he was a "good man, but so impressionable and open to manipulation." He was not that man. On the contrary, he was a gift to us. It was he who did us the violence of presenting to us, with all forthrightness, the gospel of Jesus, and he who has inspired us by his own example to receive the heavy burden of that gospel, which becomes light as it is shouldered.

I should like to conclude by asking God to make the spirit of Archbishop Romero more and more present and effective among us. If we follow in his footsteps we shall further the cause of justice and peace, truth and love; we shall help denounce atrocities, destruction, and repression; we shall help to shorten and humanize our wars; we shall defend the cause of the poor throughout the world—and certainly, in El Salvador, we shall defend the cause of a people that Archbishop Romero loved so much that he gave his life for them.

March 24, 1983

Chapter 6

Good News from God to the Poor*

Dear Brothers and Sisters:

I wish to speak to you about Archbishop Romero, whom you knew and honored at this same university five years ago. With him, I am happy to say, I bring you the finest fruit of the Salvadoran people and church: their faith, their hope, their commitment, and their martyrdom. In order to speak of Archbishop Romero today and make him present among us, I can think of nothing more helpful than *to comment briefly on the gospel that we have read.* The passage is a familiar one. Forty days after his birth, *Jesus is brought to the temple by his parents,* in accordance with the law. Let me just set this scene in its New Testament perspective, briefly, so that it may help us to a better understanding of what it really tells us about Jesus, as well as what it can tell us about Archbishop Romero.

The main thing the gospel wants to do here is "introduce" Jesus to us, "present" him to us, and not merely give us information about an event in his life. And this presentation, this introduction, places Jesus in the temple at Jerusalem, *the center of Israel's public life,* where decisions for good and ill — often enough for ill, where that people's poor were concerned — de-

*Homily delivered in the church of the University of Louvain, February 2, 1985, on the fifth anniversary of the conferral on Archbishop Romero of the honorary doctorate in theology by that university. First published in *Sal Terrae,* February 1985, pp. 161–68.

cisions on religion and faith, politics and economics, life and
death were made. Here in the temple, where his fate would be
decided when he came to the end of his life, Jesus is presented
to us as *a person of this world,* and a person in the midst of this
world. And we are asked to take a stance before him. For in
Jesus' presence, hearts will be divided. Before him, some will
fall and others rise. None will remain indifferent. Those unwilling to accept him will put him to death, and a sword of
sorrow will pierce his mother's heart.

But the solemnity of the framework, and the seriousness with
which his fate is prophesied, find their most profound purpose
in a concern to tell us *what,* above and before all else, *Jesus is.*
Two aged persons, representatives of the hopes of their people,
tell us with joy: Jesus is *"salvation,"* a *"light to the nations,"* the
"pride of his people." This is what this gospel really tells us: that
Jesus is *God's good news.* But he was not good news for all, or
for all equally. He was good news for those who, like Simeon
and Anna, *"awaited the liberation of Israel."*

This is what the gospel tells us, and this is what Jesus was:
good news. And this is *what Archbishop Romero was.* I hope that
these words do not sound like a pious exaggeration, or rhetorical
phraseology—or especially, like a voluntaristic attempt to my-
thologize Archbishop Romero after his death. I speak them with
the deepest conviction, and sincere gratitude.

If I may be permitted a very personal reflection: I have often
asked myself *what Archbishop Romero really was,* and how I might
sum up, in a single phrase, all the richness of his life. Archbishop
Romero was doubtless a matchless prophet, in whom the word
of God flowed like limpid waters, revealing hearts like a two-
edged sword, sternly denouncing oppressors and tenderly defending the oppressed. In him the poor recognized the truth of
their silence, and proclaimed him the "voice of the voiceless."
He was also the lucid teacher, who lighted up his people's path,
teaching them so clearly, and learning from the poor with such
humility. Of him they could say: "This teacher, at least, teaches
with authority." He was a shepherd who maintained solidarity
with his people to the end, refusing to keep his life for himself,
like the hireling, but delivering it up as the good shepherd, for
his flock. The poor therefore celebrate him as their martyr. In

all things he was a brother, close to his people, compassionate, as today's reading from the Letter to the Hebrews says, someone who guided his people to salvation not from on high, but, like the true high priest, from below, sharing their tears and uttering their cries. Like Jesus, Archbishop Romero "was not ashamed to call brothers" the poor of his people, and they regarded him as genuinely theirs, and therefore called him simply *Monseñor,* without further qualification, without having to add his name — he was the bishop, the shepherd, par excellence.

This is what Salvadorans saw and touched with their hands over the course of three years. It was their experience that, through his word to them and his defense of them, through his familiarity with them and his accompaniment of their quest, Archbishop Romero was good to them. They experienced him with the pride of Salvadorans, and the gratitude of believers. It is no exaggeration, therefore, to assert that Archbishop Romero was God's good news to the poor. As Father Ellacuría said shortly after Archbishop Romero's martyrdom, "With Archbishop Romero, God has visited El Salvador."

Thus, I think, Archbishop Romero ought to be presented, introduced, as Jesus was presented to those who awaited the salvation of their people — as a gift of good news from on high to the poor of this world.

But precisely for this reason — since this homily is not intended as a panegyric on Archbishop Romero, who needs none, but because, as believers, we care about the presence of God in this world, and as human beings we care about the hope of the poor of the earth — in view of what Archbishop Romero was for his people, then, we ought to ask ourselves what has become of him. Or more precisely, what have we done with him? What is left of this divine visitation to El Salvador?

Thus I should like to ask three simple questions: *Where* is Archbishop Romero alive today? *How* does Archbishop Romero live today? And *why* is Archbishop Romero still alive today?

Where Is Archbishop Romero Alive Today?

In order to answer this first question, we need only allow our gaze to wander over the multitudes of the Salvadoran people.

In their shelters, in the base communities of poor believers, in the parishes, in the religious communities of those who work with all of these other communities, a portrait, a poster—or, among the very poorest, a faded photograph clipped from a newspaper—of Archbishop Romero is always there. In their liturgical celebrations, in the meetings in which they decide what to do, what to say to God, what difficulties to try to overcome and what commitments to take up, where to find the strength for forgiveness and reconciliation—the memory of Archbishop Romero is always fresh and alive. In the Sunday homilies in the cathedral there is always emotional applause at the mention of his name.

All of these outward signs are the expression of something more profound. Archbishop Romero lives *in the hearts of the poor and crucified,* and in the hearts of *those who have cast their lot with them.* He lives where the great decisions are made for an option between despair and hope, between the complicity of indifference and toil, between selfishness and the generous gift of self unto the very surrender of one's life. This is where Archbishop Romero lives. Amidst a world caught up in a struggle between life and death, he lives among those who are on the side of life, because they love life, need life, and desire to bestow it on others. He does not live among those indifferent to the life and death of the Salvadoran people, and who therefore either ignore Archbishop Romero or vouchsafe to accord him token praise. Nor does he live among those who have taken sides with death, and who therefore continue to attack him. He lives in the poor of this world, who still hope for the good news of their liberation, and are still in love with the prophet who proclaimed it to them with such credibility. Archbishop Romero lives where he has always lived: in the poor of his people.

How Does Archbishop Romero Live Today?

The life of Archbishop Romero today is like that of Jesus. It is a resurrected life. Archbishop Romero is *risen from the dead.* That is, he lives by pouring his spirit into the Salvadoran people.

Archbishop Romero's spirit is first of all a spirit of *truth,* as he continues to be *light* for us who seek and proclaim the truth of our country and refuse to allow it to be subjected to the lie, manipulation, or propaganda of vested interests. Therefore those who tell the truth about our land, proclaim its agony, and press for a rapid resolution of our conflict, a resolution based on justice and truth, live by his spirit. Those who continue to lend their voice to the suffering of a whole people, those who give utterance to the most profound, however subjugated, truth of the poor, those who steadfastly remain the voice of those voiceless depositories of the truth, the poor—all of these live by his spirit.

Archbishop Romero's spirit is a spirit of *hope,* as well. To be honest with the truth of our land, and to maintain hope there, would seem an all but impossible task. How can we ever prevent all our war, destruction, repression, kidnapings, disappearances, murders, and tortures? How can we ever achieve peace—rebuild a country now fallen twenty years behind through its impoverishment? How can a million refugees and displaced persons ever be returned to their hearth and home? How can we come to be a Salvadoran people? To maintain this hope would seem an all but impossible task, and it is surely an affair of spirit—much spirit. But in El Salvador the stubbornness of hope endures. The poor continue to hope and toil for their liberation. The spirit of Archbishop Romero is alive in them. They have taken to heart his words of hope: "Upon these ruins shall shine the glory of the Lord!" And amidst a poor and impoverished people, the spirit of Archbishop Romero continues to engender life.

Archbishop Romero is alive as a *spirit of freedom and creativity.* Like the risen Jesus, he has not been transformed into a law—into a dead letter or a paralyzing orthodoxy. He lives in the creativity of his followers, and not in the perfunctory praise of those who only pretend to respect him. Those who seek to humanize our conflict, and are willing to go to any lengths to initiate a genuine national dialogue in behalf of the poor, are creatively reproducing his humanizing spirit of dialogue. Archbishop Romero's spirit demonstrates its freedom and creativity especially in the communities of the poor. After his martyrdom, how many Christians of these communities stood motionless, like the disciples after the Ascension, gazing up toward heaven, looking for the miracle of Archbishop Romero's return! Now they have accepted the fact that Archbishop Romero must be followed without the benefit of his physical presence. They have overcome their first fear and confusion. And these communities are growing, seeking and finding new pathways of evangelization, new tasks to perform, and new commitments. Archbishop Romero's spirit is present because it continues to *inspire Salvadorans to build the Reign of God* in a new history, a history in such urgent need of peace, humanization, and justice.

Why Is Archbishop Romero Still Alive Today?

Finally, let us ask what, I should think, is the most fundamental question of all: Why is Archbishop Romero still alive today? In all humility, Archbishop Romero stated: "If they kill me, I shall rise again in the Salvadoran people." Why have those words been fulfilled?

The best explanation, once more, is *Jesus' resurrection.* When Peter presented the risen Jesus to the Gentiles, he summed up his earthly life in these words: "He went about doing good." When we speak of Archbishop Romero's resurrection today, we must repeat these words. To the Salvadoran people, Archbishop Romero is one who went about doing good, and who intended nothing other than the good of his people. That is, Archbishop Romero had a great love for his people, an immense love for them, and this is why he is still alive in his poor.

Such love is not an everyday thing. Among decent persons we frequently encounter some interest in the poor; but it is a halfhearted love. Again, we frequently encounter a genuine love for the poor, but a love accompanied by personal or partisan interests, perhaps altogether legitimate interests. But we rarely encounter a love for one's people unmixed with anything else: a love that not only is totally forgetful of self, but which relativizes even the institutional church—precisely as institutional—that one represents, as one risks one's life, and the platforms and structures of the church, for the love of one's people. This is what the Salvadoran people have experienced: a truly great love, the love of someone who really *loved them and gave them all that he possessed.*

In Archbishop Romero, Salvadorans have seen someone who

heard the cry of an oppressed people, and who did all that in him lay to deliver them; who pleaded for structural changes, who *encouraged the poor to organize,* who judged any political solution by the sole *criterion of the good of the poor.* They have seen someone who came upon a victim lying along the side of the road — a whole crucified people — and who did not thereupon take the long way around, but who did everything he could to bind their wounds, as he opened the first shelters and organized a pastoral ministry of social work. They have seen someone who, in the presence of concrete oppression, denounced the oppressors by their very names, and announced the names of their victims — to whom he restored their dignity at least in death; who championed the Archdiocesan Legal Assistance in its efforts to denounce violations of human rights and defend the poor.

But Archbishop Romero's great love was shown not only in his defense of the poor. It was also shown in his identification with them, to the very cross. As their archbishop, he addressed to them these terrible words, so consistent with everything else he said and did: "I rejoice, brothers and sisters, that our church is persecuted precisely for its preferential option for the poor, and for seeking to become incarnate in the interests of the poor." And lest there remain the slightest doubt about his solidarity with these poor, he added: "How sad it would be, in a country where such horrible murders are being committed, if there were no priests among the victims! A murdered priest is a testimonial of a church incarnate in the problems of the people." And he said the same of himself, in all serenity, as threats against his life suddenly mounted: "A shepherd seeks no security as long as the flock is threatened."

But he not only identified with his people; he *trusted his people.* As their archbishop, before writing important documents, he seriously asked the communities of the poor what they themselves thought — they, the poor, whose opinion no one ever asks — on matters of basic concern to the country, the church, and the faith. Again as their archbishop, he even went so far as to tell them:

> If they ever take our radio, suspend our newspaper, silence us, put to death all of us priests, bishop included, and you

are left alone — a people without priests — then each of you will have to be God's microphone. Each of you will have to be a messenger, a prophet.

He was their archbishop, and yet he learned from these poor, and permitted himself to be evangelized by them.

And he had not only confidence in his poor, his people; he took *joy and pride in his people.* How often he went out to the villages and districts, as Jesus did, to encounter the poor, the small, children, and the aged, to chat with them, to celebrate the eucharist with them, to feel their human warmth and their tenderness "up close," to share their problems and their humble table! There Archbishop Romero's heart took its rest. Like Jesus, Archbishop Romero felt a sense of jubilation when the poor understood the mystery of the Reign of God. With great humility, and great joy, he could say: "With this people, it is no trouble to be a good shepherd. . . . To me this service is a deeply satisfying duty."

Such was Archbishop Romero's love for his people. He placed all that he had at the service of the liberation of the poor, identified with them, trusted them, rejoiced and suffered with them, and was proud of them. By reason of that great love, he continues to be present among them.

But likewise by reason of that love, so many persons were able to go through Archbishop Romero to something beyond him. Through his concrete, historical love he made God's love present; through his person he made Jesus present; and this has enabled the *faith* of the poor, as of so many others, to *grow,* like a luxuriant tree. Again by reason of that love, so many have understood, and made progress in, love, compassion, and justice as the way to be a Christian or even simply a human being in today's world. How many persons have come to support the cause of the poor, risking their possessions and their very lives for that cause! And in it all, what deep meaning and joy they have found for their lives!

This is what I should like to say to you in stating that Archbishop Romero was, and is, good news — a gospel of God for the world of today. But before returning to the altar I should like to add one more thing. Like any gospel, Archbishop Romero is also demanding and challenging. Standing in his presence, and being, because of his presence, in the presence of the gospel of Jesus, we must take a position. It is not enough to receive good news gratefully. One must *put it into action,* cost what it may. And today we must put the good news that is Archbishop Romero into action. Our Latin American situation continues to require this.

Not only has the situation in El Salvador not improved since Archbishop Romero's martyrdom; it has actually deteriorated. Five million human beings are in the throes of a brutal civil war. One million of these are refugees or displaced persons. More than sixty thousand families mourn their loved ones, who have been arrested, made to "disappear," been tortured, kidnapped, murdered, or have fallen in combat. The tragedy is immense, and there is no end in sight. And not only in El Salvador, but among so many other peoples, the lives of human beings — God's creation, God's children — are threatened and debased.

In life Archbishop Romero uttered his famous cry: "In the name of God: Stop the repression!" Today he would surely say, and even more forcefully: "In the name of God, and in the name of this suffering people, whose screams and cries mount to heaven, and daily grow louder, I beg you, I entreat you, I order you in the name of God: Stop the repression, stop the war, stop the bombings, stop the destruction, stop the intervention! Let us begin to build! Let us begin to live together as brothers and sisters!"

Dear brothers and sisters: These are the demands made of us today by Archbishop Romero, by the gospel of Jesus, and by the God of life. In El Salvador, as among so many other crucified peoples, the part of the great task of liberation that falls to us is represented by these words of his (and we beg the grace to be faithful to them): "I shall not abandon my people." Your part of this same enterprise — yours and that of all the churches and peoples that have such great resources at their disposition — your part in this enterprise is to hear and obey those other words of his, uttered shortly before he died, when he was asked what could be done for El Salvador: "Do not forget that we are human beings!"

To those who ignore the tragedy of the poor, Archbishop

Romero continues to say: Do not forget the millions of the daughters and sons of God who continue to suffer in this world. To those who have entered into solidarity with them, he speaks words of encouragement, urging them to keep on with their solidarity, which is so necessary, so indispensable, and we thank them with all our hearts. To all, to you and to us, Archbishop Romero continues to offer his challenge and his good news.

God grant that we may all be transformed into good news for the poor of this world. They will restore it to us with interest. God grant that the spirit of Archbishop Romero seize us in this eucharist, in our lives, and in our history, that thus we may be able to share ourselves like the bread in which Jesus will shortly become present, and so be able to distribute it to all and share it with all, making the Reign of God present in our world. In this way—together with Archbishop Romero and so many other men and women like him—we shall be faithful followers of Jesus, and walk together as a single people toward the Father of all.

February 5, 1985

Notes

1. For the full Spanish text of certain key documents by Archbishop Romero — including the Louvain address, the four pastoral letters, and the Georgetown address — see Jon Sobrino, Ignacio Martín-Baró, and R. Cardenal, *La voz de los sin voz* (San Salvador: UCA Editores, 1980). For English translations of the full text of the above-named key documents and other works by Archbishop Romero, see *Voice of the Voiceless: The Four Pastoral Letters and Other Statements* (Maryknoll, N.Y.: Orbis Books, 1985). In the present work, citations of statements or writings by Archbishop Romero were translated from the author's Spanish text.

2. For the full text of the interview, see *El Diario de Caracas,* March 19, 1980.

3. Throughout the present book, dates that stand alone in parentheses or brackets refer to the date of a homily by Archbishop Romero.

4. It is important to recall the complexity of Archbishop Romero as a person, since he excelled, as well, as a "shepherd," and therefore was also possessed of a second charism which bears analysis. In analyzing his propheticism, then, I fail to express the whole wealth of his figure and work; but I do express an important aspect in that figure and work — indeed, a surprising one, since propheticism and ecclesiastical office do not usually go hand in hand.

5. Most of my citations are from these homilies, since they are the best expression of his prophetic content, and even more, of his prophetic style. The ellipses in these texts sometimes indicate the applause with which those assisting responded to his homilies.

6. Puebla says: "The truth is that there is an ever increasing distance between the many who have little and the few who have much" (see no. 2 of the Final Document in *Puebla and Beyond,* ed. John Eagleson and Philip Scharper [Maryknoll, N.Y.: Orbis Books, 1979], p. 117).

7. Thus spoke Father Rutilio Grande, another of the great Salvadoran prophets, in his homily in Apopa, February 13, 1977, a month before his assassination.

8. All quotations in this chapter are from Archbishop Romero, whether or not indicated as such in the text.

9. *Monseñor Oscar Arnulfo Romero* (San Salvador: Publicaciones del Arzobispado), p. 1.